AVERY CARDOZA'S
CASINO ™

Strategy Guide

This book is dedicated to the "founding fathers" of
Cardoza Entertainment - Tenzing, Mike, Brian, Janet, Adam and Rich

ABOUT THE AUTHOR

Avery Cardoza is the foremost gambling authority in the world and the best-selling author of more than a dozen gambling books and advanced strategies including the encyclopedic *How to Win at Gambling*, and the best-selling classic, *Winning Casino Blackjack for the Non-Counter.*

Though originally from New York City, where he is occasionally found, Cardoza has used his winnings to pursue a lifestyle of extensive travelling which has included extended sojourns in such exotic locales as Bahia, Jerusalem and Tokyo, as well as parts of California, South Florida, New Orleans, and of course, Las Vegas, where he did extensive research into the mathematical, emotional and psychological aspects of winning.

Cardoza Publishing, publisher of **Gambling Research Institute** (GRI) books, is the foremost gaming and gambling publisher in the world with a library of more than 75 up-to-date and easy-to-read books and strategies.

These authoritative works are written by the top experts in their fields and with more than 5,000,000 books in print, represent the best-selling and most popular gaming books anywhere.

To get a complete 32 page color catalogue from Cardoza Publishing, write: Cardoza Publishing, 132 Hastings Street, Brookly, NY 11235

AVERY CARDOZA'S
CASINO ™
Strategy Guide

AVERY CARDOZA

- Gambling Research Institute -
Cardoza Publishing

CARDOZA ENTERTAINMENT'S LIMITED 90 DAY WARRANTY
For Full Warranty, send in your Registration Card Now!

CUSTOMER SUPPORT DEPARTMENT - (619)794-9178

Before calling technical support, read both the TROUBLESHOOTING and the README.txt sections; or check our web site at WWW.CardozaEnt.com - the answers to your questions most likely will lie there. If not, you may call our tech support number, 10:00-5:00 Pacific Standard Time, Monday to Friday.

Limitations

System Requirements

IBM-compatible 486/66Mhz (or greater) with 8MBram. (Pentium recommended.) Microsoft Windows 3.1 or Windows 95, 256 color SVGA, Windows-compatible mouse, Double Speed CD-ROM, Sound Blaster-compatible sound card.

INTERESTING FACTS ABOUT THE GAME

If you're wondering why *Avery Cardoza's Casino* is so much richer than anything you've seen before, a few of the facts below may clue you in. One fact however, not in this list ,stands above all. We respect and take pride in the work we do, and respect our customers who will be playing the game. We want you to *really* like our game.

As you will soon discover, many of the animations will be seen only once in a blue moon, and a few, that will only appear on the green moons. Dozens are so rare that you will be lucky to see them more than a few times a year. We've also loaded the games with surprises - we're not telling - you'll just have to keep on playing for months and months and months to even *attempt* to see them all.

Here's the facts.

• Cardoza Entertainment worked 27 months developing *Avery Cardoza's Casino*, more than 33 months including planning and design.
• More than 31 man years are invested in the game's development.
• The game cost more than $1,000,000 to produce
• This is the only casino simulation game ever created with talking interactive dealers with this level of responsiveness, artificial intelligence and huge amount of animations. More than 255 criteria trigger off 1803 different responses.
• There are more than 260,000 cells of information in the statistics comprised of 507 information fields by 25 sessions plus one cumulative totals session by 20 player memory. In short, that's a lot!
• The Ask the Expert advice gives exact correct moves to more than 1,000,000 unique possibilities. (Actually the figure is over one billion, but we thought one million might be easier to comprehend!)
• The Instruction Mode covers advice for every situation in every game.
• There are over 19 million lines of compiled C++ code in the game.
• The game contains 11,876 individually *hand-enhanced* frames of animation and 3344 sound files including both dialogue and sound effects.
• Avery, Tenzing, and Mike, by agreement, did not cut their hair until the entire production process was finished and the game shipped. (Their hair got long.)

Check out our web site at:
www.CardozaEnt.com

Important!
Send in Your Registration Card Now!

Avery Cardoza's Casino Credits

Game Conception and Design
Tenzing Kernan
Avery Cardoza

Programming Director
Michael R. Perry

Programming
Michael R. Perry
Adam K. Krist

Additional Programming
David Anderson

Art Director
Brian Kramer

3-D Modeling and Animation
Brian Kramer

2-D Artwork and Backgrounds
Janet Rucci
Joe Caporale

Executive Producer
Tenzing Kernan

Associate Producer
Richard Hutchins

Gambling Strategies and Statistics
Avery Cardoza

Sound Effects/Voice Over Editing
Mike Laughbaum

Character Dialogue
Tenzing Kernan

Character Voices
Mike Dale
Mike Laughbaum
Carole Brummage

Casino Strategy Guide
Avery Cardoza

Game Testing & Product Support
Richard Diaz
Shaun Bryant

Game Instructions
Avery Cardoza
Richard Hutchins

Box Design and Layout
Avery Cardoza
Brian Kramer
Janet Rucci

Special Thanks
Tri Synergy, Inc.
Tamra Nestler
Lix Oxley
Shaun Nestler
Julian Silberstang

TABLE OF CONTENTS

GAME INSTRUCTIONS SECTION

GAMING & STRATEGY SECTION

GAME INSTRUCTIONS SECTION

INTRODUCTION

You have purchased a state-of-the-art product that has completely pushed the limit of today's technology. One million dollars, 27 months, and 31 man years of development went into the product you now hold in your hands.

In all, our incredible creative team has created more game variations, animations, reaction criteria, sound and learning tools than any casino simulation every created. If it says, "Cardoza Entertainment" on the box, you know you're getting the best product money can buy from a company that cares about what they produce.

Look for some great upcoming games - *Avery Cardoza's Slots* (with 100 slot machines), *Avery Cardoza's Blackjack*, and *Avery Cardoza's Poker*. We'll allways bring you the best.

Enjoy the game, good skill and be a winner! And check out our web site at www.Cardozaent.com for the latest info on upgrades, new products, specials, free gambling information, and more!

HOW TO ENJOY YOUR GAME MORE

There may be a tendency when playing our game for you to make enormous bets you would never normally make if it was *real* money at stake. But that's the great fun of our casino simulation - you can play with sums of money you would never dream of doing in real life.

However, if you want to use *Avery Cardoza's Casino* as an experience that more closely resembles your own reality, we've given you three bankroll choices when registering - $200, $500, and $2,500 - so that you may more closely simulate your actual gaming experience. Our goal in this game is not only to give you the closest simulation possible to the real thing, and to have you enjoy the game to its fullest extent, but also to make you a better player. It's always more fun to be a winner, so hopefully this feature gets you ready for intelligent play when you find yourself in a real casino.

INSTALLATION

1. Place *Avery Cardoza's Casino* CD in your CD-ROM drive.

2. *If you are using Windows 3.1x*, choose "Run" from the File menu in Program Manager and type **D:\setup** at the command line, with "D" being the Drive letter of your CD-ROM drive. Click **OK** to start the setup program.

3. *If you are using Windows 95* you can go to Add/Remove programs in the control panel and select install. Windows95 will detect the installation program and ask if you want to continue or you can select Run from the Start menu and type **D:\setup** with "D" being the drive letter of your CD-ROM drive. Click **OK** to start the setup program.

4. The Setup wizard will start. To install the game in the default directories and program groups, click the **Next** button at each screen of the installation and select **Yes** when prompted for the creation of new directories and folders. This is the easiest way to install the game.

5. If you wish, you may change the directory that the casino files will be installed to. Click the **Next** button when you satisfied with the directory path and select **Yes** if asked to confirm its creation. The default directory is **C:\Cardoza\Casino**.

6. Setup Type Options

Typical Installation:
Selecting typical installation will install the Casino program files onto your hard drive. A Typical installation uses the least amount of your hard disk space, about 15 MB. You

will need to have the CD in the drive to play the game using this type of installation.

Complete Installation:

A complete installation will install all of the Casino program and data files onto your hard drive. Selecting the complete installation improves the performance of the game at the cost of using a great deal of hard disk space (about 340 MB).

Custom Installation:

Selecting the custom installation will open a dialogue box that will allow you to install selected games on your hard drive. The performance of games installed on the hard drive will be improved, particularly the dealer games - blackjack, craps and roulette. If running a slower machine, or you have a slow CD-ROM, we recommend that you install your favorite dealer game for optimal performance.

You will still need the CD in the drive to start the game unless you install the Casino and Lobby files in addition to any games you want on your hard drive.

 If you decide to remove or add areas of the casino at a later time you should first uninstall the casino using the uninstall icon in the casino's program folder.

6. If you wish, you may select a different program folder or create a new program folder for the Casino icons to be placed in. The default folder name for Cardoza Entertainment products is **"Cardoza Entertainment**." If you are using Windows 95, then the folder name selected will be added to the program list in your start menu. Click the **Next** button when you are satisfied with the Folder name and select **Yes** if asked to confirm its creation.

7. Once the files have been installed, the setup program will display some basic instructions on getting started. Click the **Next** or **Back** button to scroll through these screens. At the Setup finish screen, we recommend that you look at the Casino Readme.txt file for any last minute information; then you can start the game.

8. *To start the game in Windows 3.1x* after the setup program has closed, double-click the *Avery Cardoza's Casino* Icon in the **Cardoza Entertainment** program folder.

To start the game in Windows 95 after the setup program has closed click the Start button and select Programs, click the Cardoza Entertainment folder and select *Avery Cardoza's Casino* from the list. **Cardoza Entertainment** is the default program folder used by the setup program, if you changed the folder name during installation the program icons will be located in the folder you designated.

How Much Space Do You Need to Install Avery Cardoza's Casino?

A typical installation requires about 15MB of hard drive space, and a complete installation about 330MB. Custom installation requirements are determined by the areas that you select: Slots will take up about 100MB, Blackjack 50MB, Craps 60MB, Roulette 40MB, Video Poker 45MB and Keno about 2MB. (Other casino files will use about 30MB).

Loading Time

You will experience a little bit of a loading wait when the game is first turned on due to the very large number of animations in the game and the sophisticated nature and depth of this game. We elected to put the wait time up front in the loading stage, as opposed to in the game itself, so you could derive maximum pleasure from the use of this product. Also, expect a small wait when changing games within the casino for the same reason. Then knock 'em dead!

TROUBLESHOOTING

Game Is Cut Off at the Bottom

• No Sweat. Hit the ESC (Escape) key for the full screen to appear. Click Esc or the Menu button to re-access Windows menu.

Can't Access the Windows Menu

• In a 640 x 480 mode your game will appear on the full screen. To access the Window menu, hit the Menu button or the ESC (Escape) key.

Game Isn't Full Screen

• The game will only be at full screen when your monitor is set to 640 x 480 mode. Newer laptops typically ship with higher resolution settings and don't allow you the flexibility to go to a 640 x 480 mode. However, most home computers can be reset to 640 x 480 in the following manner:

Computers Running Windows 95:

• Right mouse click anywhere on the screen outside the game or other program. Now click on the "Properties" and then "Settings" within that window. In the Desktop area, you may see your monitor listed as 800 x 600, 1024 x 800, or some other setting. Change this to 640 x 480, close the windows, and your game will now appear full screen. To reset the setting, do the same steps as above, and change to your old setting.

Computers Running Windows 3.1x:

• A program called a video driver was installed on your computer at the time it was built. Windows uses this program to communicate with your computers' video card and monitor. The video driver program on your computer was written by the manufacturer of the video card in your computer. Consult the video card documentation that came with your computer for instructions on how to change the resolution and color setting of your display. *Avery Cardoza's Casino* works best on systems at 640 x 480 screen resolution displaying 256 colors.

No Sound

• You may have turned off the sound. Once you turn off the sound, it stays off until you turn it back on. Click on the OPTIONS menu at the top of your game screen. If the "Sound" command does not have a check mark next to it, the sound is turned off. Select the Sound Option to turn the sound back on.

• If the sound is turned on in the game but is still not working, check to see that your speakers are turned on and plugged into the speaker or output jack in your computer. Also, if there is one, check the volume knob next to the jack or on your speakers. Most computers control the volume through software. On a Windows 95 system, the software volume control is located at the lower right hand corner of you screen and looks like a speaker.

Player's Name Isn't Accessible in the Name Bar

• Your player needs to be activated. Go to CREATE/DELETE GAMBLER under the FILE menu, highlight the player's name by clicking on it, and click the ACTIVATE button. Or simply double click on the name. An aserisk (*) will appear next to active players names. Click DONE and return to the game. Note that only three players may be active at one time.

The Game Beeps and Won't Allow You to Make a Play

• The Instruction Mode may be on (it will have a check mark next to it), and you'll need to turn it off. To deactivate the Instruction Mode and return to the regular playing mode, select INSTRUC-TION MODE under the Ask Expert Window. This will toggle the feature off and allow you regular play.

Cannot Increase Bet Amount

• You are either out of money or have reached the $100,000 betting limit. If you are out of money, select CREATE/DELETE GAMBLER from the File menu.

• You have tried to make a bet that exceeds the cash you have. Can't do partner.

Windows 95 Start Menu Toolbar Buttons are Interfering with Game Buttons at Bottom of Screen.

• Right click on the toolbar and select properties. Turn the "Always on Top" and "Autohide" options off.

When You Start the Game, a Message Says You Need to Use 256 Colors to Run the Program

• The video driver that is installed is running at a color resolution other than 256 colors. If at 16 colors it must be set to 256 colors. Higher resolutions will work, but will slow game play.

Don't Know How to Play the Games?

• If you don't know the rules of play, read the *Gaming and Strategy Section* starting on page 49, or consult the on-line help file for the particular game in question.

• If you know how to play a particular game, but don't know how it works in *Avery Cardoza's Casino*, this section will explain the basics of play. You can also consult the on-line help file.

Can't Make a Bet

• In blackjack, craps and roulette, check to see that you have a bet amount entered in the BET UNIT box. If the number is 0, you need to press on any of the six bet keys: 1, 5, 25, 100, 1,000 and 10,000, to enter a bet amount. You may now bet.

• In craps, you will not be able to make a pass line bet after a point is established - it can only be made on the come-out roll. You can tell that a point has been established because the round marker ON buck will be on one of the point numbers: 4, 5, 6, 8, 9, or 10.

Similarly, you won't be able to make come and don't come bets on the come-out roll; they can only be made while a point is established.

• In all games, check to see that you have enough money left in your bankroll to make the bet or that you're not bankrupt. No bucks, no play baby. Go to CREATE/DELETE GAMBLER under the FILE menu to make a new gambler and get more dough. Since you've already gone dry, you'll need to create a new name.

Cannot Delete a Gambler

• Make sure the gambler's name is highlighted, then click the DELETE button.

• Only deactivated gamblers may be deleted. If the gambler has an asterisk (*) next to his or her name, click on the name and then the DEACTIVATE button, or double click until the asterisk is removed. You may now delete the gambler.

• Note that if Joe Gambler gets deleted, he immediately gets recreated with a $500 bankroll.

Cannot Create a Gambler

• You may have exceeded the maximum limit of 20 gamblers. Remove one gambler for each gambler you wish to add.

Cannot Activate a Gambler

• Make sure the gambler's name is highlighted, then click the ACTIVATE button. An asterisk will appear next to the name.

• You already have three active gamblers. You must deactivate one gambler to be able to activate another.

CD Drive Won't Read the CD. It Says "Cannot Read Drive"

Make sure the CD is clean and properly seated in the drive. Also, make sure that you have the correct drivers for your CD drive installed. Test the CD drive with another CD to verify the problem is not with the drive.

IV. OPTIMIZING PERFORMANCE

If you find that your game runs too slow for your taste, and would like to speed up and optimize its' performance, the following tips will probably solve the problem.

INSTALL FAVORITE DEALER GAME TO THE HARD DRIVE

If you have a slower CD ROM, you should consider installing your favorite dealer game, blackjack, craps, or roulette, to the hard drive (choose CUSTOM under installation) for the best performance. The other games, slots, video poker, and roulette, will run relatively fast off the CD ROM on most machines. In all cases, the games will play best running off the hard drive.

If you have already loaded the game, and wish to now install one of the dealer games, you'll first need to use the "uninstall" program in the game folder on your desktop or start menu if you're using Windows95, and then reisnstall the program using the CUSTOM option (see installation instructions on page 12-14).

To run the uninstall program, double click the icon that reads "uninstall."

INCREASE YOUR RAM

Avery Cardoza's Casino will perform better on computers with more RAM available for the game. With RAM so inexpensive nowadays, you may want to consider bumping it up to improve the overall performance of your computer anyway.

We recommend that you have at least 16 MB of RAM for best results and playability. If your machine, has just 8MB, and you do upgrade it to 16 MB, you'll notice a tremendous improvement in the game's performance.

CLOSE DOWN OTHER PROGRAMS

Close all other Windows applications when you play *Avery*

Cardoza's Casino for improved performance.

TABLE GAME SPEED CONTROL:
BLACKJACK, CRAPS, ROULETTE

The GAME SPEED CONTROL option, available under the OPTIONS menu, adjusts the levels of animations and sounds in the game so that you can achieve the optimum balance between game richness and speed. Thus, if you have a slow computer, you may want to choose the FAST or FASTEST setting, while if you have a fast computer, you'll enjoy the fullest experience with the RICHEST setting.

RICHEST (recommended) - This setting will provide the richest game experience and is highly recommended. This works best with fast machines.

RICH - This setting will cause the dealer to be slightly less talkative than at the richest setting.

FAST - This setting will provide a quicker game flow for players who want more action and less chatter.

FASTEST (for slow machines) - This setting is recommended for computers which run slowly on all of the other settings. will result in super fast game flow.

GAME INSTRUCTIONS

INTRODUCTION

This section shows how to play the various games in *Avery Cardoza's Casino*. See the second part of this book, the *Gaming and Strategy Section*, for information on the rules and basics of play for each of the games, as well as strategy information on being a winner!

WINDOWS MENU

To access the Windows menu at the top of your screen when you're in 640 x 480 full screen mode, hit the ESC key or click on the MENU button. Click anywhere on the game screen to return to the full screen mode.

QUICK PLAY INSTRUCTIONS

(See Each Individual Game for Greater Detail)

1. Choose a game by clicking on its image in the lobby or selecting it from the drop down GAME menu. Allow a little time for the game to load and open.

2. You may play using the default name, "Joe Gambler," or list your own name and other active players. Only three players may be active at one time. To add players, go to CREATE/DELETE GAMBLER under FILE menu. Click CREATE GAMBLER, type in your name, then DONE. An asterisk lets you know you're active.

3. Do above for each player to be active. Remember to click on Joe Gambler and click DEACTIVATE if you don't want him listed as an active player.

4. On table games, set BET UNIT by clicking on numbered bet keys; then click on the bet spots to place wagers. Press DICE in craps, DEAL in blackjack, and SPIN in roulette to get the action going.

5. In video poker and slots, click BET ONE (then SPIN) or BET MAX. In video poker, make further selection of keeping or discarding cards by clicking on card themselves, and then click DRAW.

6. In keno, click NEW TICKET, and mark anywhere from 1-10 spots on the keno ticket by clicking on the numbers you wish to play. Click PLAY TICKET. Your ticket will be played on the next game.

CHOOSING A GAME

You have 65 varieties of games to choose from and can access them by clicking directly on them from the lobby, or from the Windows menu, by clicking on the GAME menu, and the game desired to go to another casino game. Blackjack, slots and video poker have further drop down menus which can be accessed by keeping the mouse positioned over them for about a second.

CHANGING GAMES

To change to a new game, select the game you want under the GAME menu. For example, if you're playing roulette and want to switch to blackjack, select BLACKJACK under the GAME menu and the game will open up. There's no need to actually exit any game, simply move on to the next one.

You can also access any game by returning to the lobby (click Lobby under GAME menu) and clicking on the game or machine you wish to play.

CREATING/DELETING GAMBLERS

To add gamblers to the game, open up CREATE/DELETE GAMBLER under the FILE Menu.

Your game starts with one active player, Joe Gambler. To register yourself as a player, click CREATE, and type in the information requested - your name, sex and desired starting bank-roll, then click DONE. A pop-up screen will confirm that you are activated - click OKAY - you are returned to the CREATE/DELETE GAMBLER screen. Click DONE to exit.

You are now automatically activated as a gambler. If there are three gamblers already active when you create a new gambler, the pop-up menu will tell you that the new gambler won't be active until one of the other three are deactivated. Three active gamblers are the maximum allowed.

ACTIVE AND INACTIVE PLAYERS

Active players are listed and accessible in the colored name bar when the games themselves are open. Gamblers that are not active are not listed, and therefore cannot play.

When you create and activate your name in a single or multi-player game, you may also want to deactivate "Joe Gambler." He will remain active until you deactivate him. He also remains active by default if there is no other player active and a game is open.

MAKING LISTED GAMBLERS ACTIVE OR INACTIVE

To make a gambler active, highlight his or her name by clicking on it, then click ACTIVATE, or double click on the name. An asterisk will appear next to the name indicating that the player is active and ready to play. Click DONE to return to the game.

Note that only three players may be active at one time. To add an additional player when the three player limit is reached, you'll first need to deactivate one of the active players (see below).

Players stay active even after the game is exited and restarted.

REMOVING OR DEACTIVATING PLAYERS

Removing or deactivating gamblers is also done from the CREATE/DELETE GAMBLER under the FILE Menu.

To remove an active player from the game, but keep his or her name listed (for future play or to retain their statistics), click to highlight that name, then click DEACTIVATE; or double click until the asterisk is removed. That player is now deactivated.

You may also permanently delete a player by highlighting the name with the mouse and clicking DELETE. A dialog box will pop up and ask you, "You are about to delete this gambler. Are you Sure?" Click DELETE to permanently delete, or CANCEL, if you change your mind. Since active players, those noted with an asterisk, may not be deleted, you must first deactivate the player before clicking DELETE.

A maximum of 20 players can be listed at one time. To make room for additional players, you'll first need to delete an equal number of names.

Note that if Joe Gambler gets deleted, he immediately gets recreated with a $500 bankroll.

MULTIPLE PLAYERS

To play a multi-player game, you must first have all participating players, up to three maximum allowed, registered as "active."

The players whose name appears on the button bar is the current player and may make his or her bet first. You may, instead, click on the name itself (or use the Tab key) to have another player bet first. Each click "toggles" to the next active player.

Click on Name Bar here to
toggle to next active player.

With two or three players are registered to play, clicking on the colored name area at the center of the buton bar will toggle between active players. You can also use the TAB key. Each click or tab will move to the next active player. The NAME BAR is color coded with three colors, blue, red and green, one color being assigned to each player.

The sparkle that marks the winning bets will match the color of the name bar for each player in roulette and craps, while in blackjack, the bet circles will be highlighted in that player's color. This helps players identify their wagers.

INSTRUCTION MODE

This powerful feature allows you to learn the best way to maximize your winnings *while* you play. Select ASK THE EXPERT from the Windows menu, then click INSTRUCTION MODE to activate it. A check mark will appear next to Instruction Mode.

Here's how it works. Whenever you make an incorrect play, that is, a play that deviates from the optimal way to win, the ASK EXPERT button will light up and a beep will sound.

The game will not accept the play on that first click and will give you an option to change your decision. You have been alerted that an incorrect play was made. At this point, you can either click on the ASK EXPERT button to view the expert advice, or click again and make whatever play you desire.

The Instruction Mode will stay on and be active for all games (for that player only) until you manually turn it off, even after the game is shut off and restarted, so remember to deactivate the Instruction Mode when you want to play without the expert.

BUTTON BAR

All games share the same features on the left and central sections of the button bars. We'll go over these features first.

Blackjack Example

CENTRAL BUTTON BAR AREA

MENU BUTTON

Clicking on the MENU button accesses the Windows menu for the game when you're in 640 x 480 full screen mode, and also returns you to the full screen mode when you re-click. This button will work only on monitors that are set to the 640 x 480 setting. We recommend this setting for optimal game play. On settings where the game doesn't appear full screen, the Windows menu will be accessible at all times and the MENU button will serve no function.

HELP BUTTON

Clicking on the HELP button opens up a window that gives you access to the full on-line help text of the game: game specific instructions, how to play information on the games themselves, strategies for how to win, and trouble shooting. A full table of contents, search and index gives you powerful capabilities to access anything you need from the on-line help within a matter of seconds.

The on-line Help is programmed in Hypertext so that clicking on any colored item will take you directly to that topic. You may also easily navigate through the help text by using the easy access

25

buttons on top. The CONTENTS button shows the main topics; SEARCH gives you an easy to use index that will take you right to the topic of your choice; BACK takes you to the previous screen; PRINT allows you to print; GLOSSARY gives you a list of commonly used gambling terms; << takes you to precious screens within the section; and >> takes you to the following screen.

Opening up the Help from within a game takes you directly to the information relevant to that game. From here you can access the full help text as above.

NAME BAR AREA

The NAME BAR area, centrally located in the button bar (see page 24 for illustration), indicates the current player. When two or three players are registered to play, clicking here toggles between the names. Each click will move on to the next active player. The NAME BAR is color coded with three colors, blue, red and green, to help players in a two or three player game identify their turn.

In craps and roulette, blue, red and green colored sparkles are also used to identify winning bets, while in blackjack, the bet spots are lit up by color when it is a player's turn.

LEFT BUTTON BAR AREA

STATS

The button will open up directly to the statistics of the game you are playing, or if entering from CREATE/DELETE GAMBLER, to overall stats. From this window, you can access the statistics of all of the games, all registered players (up to 20), the previous 25 sessions, the cumulative sessions, and more than 500 different fields. That's 260,000 plus cells of information! Your current session, however, won't be fully tracked until after it's concluded.

BANKROLL

The bankroll area shows your current casino bankroll at any time. Once a bet has been placed on the table, committed to a keno ticket, or deposited into a machine, it is removed from your bankroll

- it now "belongs to the game."

Won bets will be immediately credited to your bankroll in blackjack, craps, roulette, slots and video poker. However, in keno, you won't receive credit for winning tickets while you were not at the game until you actually "cash in" winnng tickets by going back into the keno game and checking on those past tickets that you bet. It's just like the casino - you must claim winning tickets.

ASK THE EXPERT

Clicking on the ASK EXPERT button opens up a window with professional advice. If there is a lot of advice for the particular situation, you'll need to click on the arrows of the scroll bar (on the right side) to scroll up or down to access more information. Click "OK" or hit your ENTER key on the keyboard to close the box and return to the game.

The ASK EXPERT button can be clicked on at any point during the game, either before bets are made, or after, to get professional advice on the best strategy to follow. The ASK EXPERT button shows you the best play to make for *every* situation in *every* game. In all more than 1,000,000 situations are covered.

RIGHT BUTTON BAR AREA

Blackjack, craps, and roulette open up with a betting interface which is described below. (In slots, video poker and keno, the right action buttons are specific to the games and will be discussed individually in their sections.)

Roulette Example

BET UNIT AND BET KEYS

You must first set a BET UNIT amount to make bets. This amount, chosen by clicking on any of the six bet keys, 1, 5, 25, 100,

1,000 and 10,000, gets displayed in the BET UNIT area on the right side of your button bar. Click on the bet buttons in any combination and as often as you like to set the amount desired.

Once a bet amount is entered in the BET UNIT area, you make bets by clicking on any of the bet spots available on in the table games. Every click of the mouse enters a BET UNIT amount on the table. If "25" was entered into the BET UNIT, then one click makes a $25 bet, two clicks makes it $50, four clicks, $100 and so on.

Once a bet has been placed, any further clicking on a bet key button automatically resets the BET UNIT to the new amount entered. For example, if you bet $10 on Red in roulette, and then click "1" in the bet keys, the BET UNIT automatically resets to $1. A click on another bet, say a split bet, makes a $1 bet there. You can also change the BET UNIT by clicking on the "CLEAR" button, which resets the BET UNIT to 0, and reentering a new amount.

In the table games, clicking on a bet spot which already has a bet will add the BET UNIT amount to the wager. Each click of the mouse will add that much more to the bet.

CLEAR BUTTON

In the table games - blackjack, craps and roulette - pressing the CLEAR button sets the BET UNIT back to 0.

REMOVE BUTTON

Click on the REMOVE BETS button on your menu bar, then on the bet itself to remove any active bet. If all bets have been removed, you may now re-bet without further ado - you're automatically returned to the betting mode. If active bets still remain on the table, reclick the REMOVE BETS button to deactivate this mode and return to the regular betting mode. When the game is in the "remove bets mode," the cursor will have an "R" next to the darkened chip stack when it appears over the layout.

With the exception of the Pass and Come bets in craps, which cannot be removed once a point has been established, and blackjack bets once the cards have been dealt, any bet may be removed at any time in the table games.

CURSORS

We have created various special cursors whose functions are described below:

 Shows that the cursor is located over a valid bet area and a bet can be placed by clicking the mouse.

 Shows that the cursor is not located over a valid bet area. You may need to move it slightly to make the bet.

 In Remove Bet mode, shows that the cursor is located over a valid bet area and will remove that bet by clicking the mouse.

 In Remove Bet mode, shows that the cursor is not located over a valid bet area. You may need to move it slightly to remove the bet.

 In keno, the crayon cursor appears when it is positioned over a ticket and a mouse click will mark either a number or game information.

 When positioned over the button bar, indicates button "hot spots" that can be clicked (though not necessarily active in current mode).

 Indicates that a button has been clicked and is currently depressed. Releasing the click returns to the above cursor.

 In the lobby, this cursor shows that it is located over a valid machine or game which can be opened by clicking with the mouse.

 In the lobby, this cursor shows that it is not located over a valid machine or game. You may need to move it slightly to open a game. Keep in mind that the tip of the cursor is the hot spot.

Turning On/Off Sound

If you wish to play *Avery Cardoza's Casino* without sound, you can turn off the sound by selecting SOUND under the OPTIONS menu. The game defaults to sound (it has a check next to the option), and will toggle to no sound. Re-selecting the SOUND option will replace the checkmark and the sound.

BLACKJACK INSTRUCTIONS

QUICK PLAY INSTRUCTIONS

1. Set BET UNIT by clicking on numbered bet keys.
2. Click on any or all of three semi-circle bet spots to place your wagers.
3. Press DEAL on the bottom right of screen. Cards will be dealt.
4. Choose playing options for each hand in turn. Hands will be played in order from screen right to screen left.

Blackjack Button Bar

HOW TO MAKE A BET

You must first set a BET UNIT amount to make bets. Once a bet amount is entered in the BET UNIT area, you place bets by clicking on one, two or all three of the white semi-circle bet spots available on the bottom of your screen, or by using the hot keys 1, 2, and 3.

REMOVING BETS

Bets on the blackjack table may be removed at any time prior to the deal. However, once the cards are dealt, bets may not be removed - the game is on!

HOW TO PLAY A HAND

Once all bets have been placed on the table, press the DEAL button in the bottom right corner of the screen. Cards will be dealt to each betting spot containing a bet.

If the dealer's upcard is an Ace, you will be asked if you want to take insurance. YES and NO buttons appear. Make your choice. If the dealer has a blackjack, he will collect lost bets and the cards, and wait for you to make a bet on the following hand.

On all other dealer upcards, and provided the dealer does not have a blackjack where he will collect lost bets as above, four buttons will appear giving you the following playing options: HIT, STAND, DOUBLE DOWN, and SPLIT. Click on your choice. If one of these options is not allowed, the appropriate button will be "greyed out" - you won't be able to choose it.

Your turn will conclude when you either choose DOUBLE DOWN, where only 1 card will be given, STAND (no more cards), when you bust (your total exceeds 21), or you get a blackjack or 21. (Note that on split aces, you'll get only one card per Ace and your turn will automatically end after the card is dealt to the 2nd Ace.)

Each betting spot will be played in turn, from screen right to screen left. When all player spots have been acted upon, the dealer will expose his hole card and draw until he gets 17 points or more. (More than 21 points is a bust of course, and all remaining players will be winners.) The dealer will pay off the winners, collect from the losers, and wait for new bets to be made.

ASK THE EXPERT

In blackjack, clicking on ASK EXPERT before bets are made gives you the count information and suggested bet size if you are counting cards. Clicking on ASK EXPERT after the cards are dealt tells you how to play the correct Basic Strategy for the cards you were dealt. For more information on winning at blackjack, read the *Gaming and Strategy Section* beginning on page 49.

CRAPS INSTRUCTIONS

Crap Button Bar

Dice Rolling
Options

HOW TO MAKE A BET

You must first set a BET UNIT amount to make bets. Once a bet amount is entered in the BET UNIT area, you place bets by clicking on any of the available bets at the craps table.

REMOVING BETS

With the exception of the Pass and Come bets, which cannot be removed once a point has been established, all bets may be removed at any time.

HOW TO PLAY THE GAME AND ROLL THE DICE

Once all bets have been placed on the table, press the DICE button in the bottom right corner of the screen to roll the dice. After each dice roll, the dealer will pay off the winning bets and collect from the losers. When he has reconciled all current bets affected by the dice, you may place additional bets and roll the dice again.

DICE ROLLING OPTIONS

We've designed two unique dice options to put you right into the action. Under the DICE button, you'll notice a smaller button. Clicking on it successively gives you four choices: RAND., HORZ., VERT., and LOOP.

RAND., short for random, gives you a random throwing style; HORZ., short for horizontal, uses the horizontal, or what we call the "Bank Shake"; VERT., short for vertical, uses the vertical, or what we call the "Railroad Shake"; and finally, LOOP, our "Loop de Loop Shake."

You also control the length of the shake before the dice are thrown. When you click on the DICE button, the shooter will keep shaking the dice until the mouse is released.

Different styles and durations of dice shakes will actually re-randomize the result of your throw continually (exactly like real dice). It's all in the throw baby. *Shake up them bones.*

THE SHOOTER

The **shooter** is the player who rolls the dice. When you're playing by yourself, you're always the shooter. If you're playing with other gamblers, the shooter will roll the dice until he or she sevens-out, that is, a seven is thrown after a point has been established. The next player in turn will then be the shooter and his or her name will appear in the "Name Area" on the button bar. Dice will be passed clockwise around the table.

Traditionally, the shooter must make a pass line or don't pass bet, however, in this game you may make any bet you like and still roll the dice.

MESSAGE BAR

As the cursor is moved over the craps layout, the message bar will display the bet that you can make by clicking on the spot and the payoffs for that bet. Wagers in craps that are not marked on the layout can be easily found this way. (See below for explanations of these other bets.)

MAKING BETS NOT CLEARLY MARKED

All craps bets are made on the areas clearly marked on the table, except for the following wagers, which are not marked on the layout. This section shows you how to place these bets.

For a full explanation of how to play craps and the bets available to you, including the bets listed below, read the *Gaming and Strategy Section* or go access the on-line help for craps.

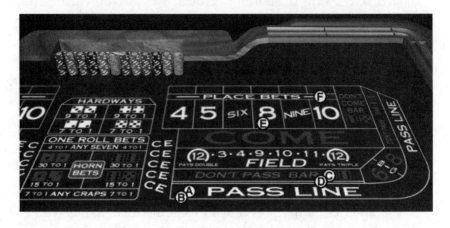

The Craps Betting Layout

A. Shows the original pass line bet.

B. Click on **"A"** to make your free odds bet. **"B"** is where your free odds will be placed.

C. Shows the original don't pass bet.

D. Click on **"C"** to make your free odds don't pass bet. **"D"** is where your free odds will be placed.

E. Click in this general location, on the lower section of the numbered box, to make place or buy bets. In this example, we are making a bet on number 8.

F. Click between these lines, and above the number you wish to bet, to make the lay bets. (You're not actually making a Place Bet as the layout might indicate.)

Taking Odds on the Pass and Don't Pass

To take free odds on these bets, click on the pass and don't pass bets themselves - these bets are only able to be made after the point has been established. Your odds bet will be placed atop the pass or don't pass bet. To place the full double odds, keep clicking on these bets until no more bets are added atop your original line bets. The game will place the maximum amount when enough money is bet and allow no more.

Taking Odds on the Come and Don't Come

Once a come point is established, the dealer moves the come bet to the upper part of the number box, and the don't come bet to the smaller upper box above the number. For example if an 8 is rolled, the come bet moves to the large rectangular box marked "8."

To take odds on these bets, you'll need to click on the chips themselves in these new locations. Your odds bets will be placed atop the come or don't come bet. To place the full double odds, keep clicking on these bets until no more chips are added to your original bets. The maximum double odds have now been bet.

TIP - PLACING THE MAXIMUM FREE ODDS BETS

To place the maximum free odds on the pass, don't pass, come or don't come bets, click repeatedly until no more chips are added to the bet. The maximum double odds have now been placed.

Place and Buy Bets

The lower half of the numbered boxes are reserved for making the place and buy bets. As you position your cursor over these areas, the message bar will indicate that the bet is valid. To make these wagers, click on the numbers you wish to bet on - 4, 5, 6, 8, 9, 10 - and the game will default to the better bet for you. Bets on the 4 and 10 will be taken as buy bets; bets on the 5, 6, 8 and 9 will be taken as place bets. You can change these defaults by choosing the appropriate item under OPTIONS (see later).

Lay Bets

The upper half of the numbered boxes are reserved for making lay bets. As you position your cursor over these areas, the message bar will indicate that the bet is valid. Click on the numbers you wish to bet against: 4, 5, 6, 8, 9, 10. Lay bets win if a 7 is rolled before that number, and lose if that number is rolled first.

All other bets are made by clicking on the area clearly marked on the layout.

CRAPS BETTING OPTIONS MENU

You have several betting options available to you in craps. To access these options drop down the OPTIONS menu at the top of the game screen and select BETTING OPTIONS. The Craps Betting Options dialogue box will appear giving you several options, described below.

PLACE/BUY
Bets on 4 and 10

You can bet numbers on the 4 and 10 directly as either a buy bet or a place bet. Since the buy bet offers better odds on these numbers, we have defaulted to it. You can change the default by clicking on the PLACE BETS option.

Buy/Place Bets on 5 and 9

You can bet numbers on the 5 and 9 directly as either a buy bet or a place bet. Since the place bet offers better odds on these numbers, we have defaulted to it. You can change the default under this menu by clicking on the BUY BETS option.

Place/Buy Bets on 6 and 8

Same explanation as above except for the 6 and 8 numbers.

BETS WORKING ON COME-OUT ROLLS
Come Bet Free Odds

It is standard for come bet free odds to be "off," not working, on the come out roll. You can override this convention by chossing "on" for this option.

Buy and Place Bets

It is standard for the buy and place odds to be "on," working, on the come out roll. You can call them "off" here.

Don't Come Free Odds

It is standard for the don't come free odds to be working on the come out roll. This option calls them "off" on the come-out.

Hardway Bets

While these bets are always working in craps, we have given you the option of turning them "off," since in essence, you would be betting against yourself as a "right" bettor.

TO ADD BETS TO EXISTING BETS

Click on the bet spot. The amount of your BET UNIT will be added to the existing bet each time you click.

CRAPS TROUBLESHOOTING

Can't Make a Pass, Don't Pass, Come, Don't Come Bets

• You will not be able to make a pass line bet after a point is established - it can only be made on the come-out roll. You can tell that a point has been established because the round marker buck will be on one of the point numbers - 4, 5, 6 8, 9, or 10. Similarly, you won't be able to make come and don't come bets on the come-out roll; they can only be made while a point is established.

Can't Make Odds Bets

• Odds bets can only be made when there is already a pass line, don't pass, come and don't come bet made, and the point for that number has been established.

Can't Make Bets in General

• Check to see that a betting amount is entered in the Bet Unit area. Bets can only be made when there is an amount greater than 0 entered in the bet unit area.

KENO INSTRUCTIONS

QUICK PLAY INSTRUCTIONS

1. Click NEW TICKET.
2. Mark anywhere from 1-10 spots on the keno ticket (to the left of the screen) by clicking on the numbers you wish to play.
3. Click PLAY TICKET, and this ticket will be played on the next game. Mark as many tickets as you like.
4. Games are automatically played every three minutes. Winning tickets will be stamped "WINNER" and your bankroll will be credited.

Keno Button Bar

INTRODUCTION

Keno games are played in our casino every three minutes, whether you're in the game or not. They run 24 hours a day, even while your computer is off! You may play tickets for up to the next 100 games, take a night out on the town or a vacation to Las Vegas, and then Hawaii, and check your results when you return. The game has a memory of the last 100,000 games played!

This history feature allows you to enjoy the faster action of the other casino games while still enjoying keno: Simply mark your tickets during breaks and return to one of the action games. Your tickets can be checked any time for wins or losses!

THE KENO BOARD

As each number is drawn, the all-powerful genie displays it in his magic ball. Twenty numbers will be drawn for each game and will appear as lighted numbers on the display. The GAME # shows the current game playing, or if the numbers have already been drawn, the one that has just been played, while the NEXT GAME display shows how much time remains until the next game begins.

HOW TO PLAY A TICKET

To make a bet, you must first mark a ticket. You do so by clicking anywhere from 1-10 spots on the blank keno ticket that appears on the lower left of the screen. The cursor will change to a crayon as you mark your numbers.

As you mark the numbers you'll play, the area below GAME will reflect the current type of ticket. For example, if you click on two spots, the GAME area will read "2." If you click a third spot, the area will now read "3," and if 7 spots are clicked, it will read "7."

After you have chosen your numbers, click on PLAY TICKET, and your bet is made for the number of spots you chose. If you had chosen 7 spots, your bet would reflect a seven spot ticket.

You may play as many tickets as you like, up to a maximum of 100. You'll need to click NEW TICKET each time to start a fresh ticket, and of course, PLAY TICKET after you've chosen your numbers and are placing the bet.

TYPES OF BETS AND PAYOFFS

You have a choice of 13 different tickets to bet; individual tickets from 1-10 spots, plus 3 spot, 4 spot, and 6 spot specials. Clicking on the word GAME on your keno ticket, or in the box below it, will show you the payoff schedule for the number of bet spots you have marked. Further clicking will show the payoffs for the other types of tickets as well.

To bet one of the three special tickets, you'll need to mark the appropriate number of spots on your ticket, then click GAME two times. The first click will show the payout schedule for the regular ticket, and the second click will show the payout for the special. Now click PLAY TICKET, and your special will get bet.

Click anywhere on the screen to re-hide the payout schedule.

PLAYING MULTIPLE GAMES

Tickets are automatically entered for 1 game. To change the number of games played with a ticket, click on the PLAYS area on the upper left of your ticket. You can play tickets for the next 1, 5, 10, 20, 50 or 100 games. Clicking in this area will toggle between these options in the listed order.

Thus, if you choose "10" games on game number 05481, your ticket will play for the following 10 games, from 05481 through 05490. On the center of the ticket itself, the games chosen will be marked in crayon and appear next to VALID ON GAMES.

CHANGING BET SIZE

Tickets are automatically entered as $1 bets. To change the bet amount played per ticket, click on the $ area on the upper right of your ticket. You can play tickets for $1, $5, or $10. Clicking in this area will toggle between the three amounts. If you are playing multiple games with this ticket (see above), the same bet will apply to all of them.

CHECKING PREVIOUS GAMES PLAYED

The display to the right of your keno ticket, marked GAME HISTORY, keeps track of the last 100,000 games played. Clicking on the right and left directional arrows changes the display to reflect older and newer games respectively. The number at the top center of the display indicates the game played, while the numbers in the diplay itself show the numbers that were drawn for that game. You can match these numbers up with older tickets played.

CHECKING PREVIOUS TICKETS PLAYED

The directional arrows at the bottom of your keno ticket allows you to check previous games to see what tickets you played and how you fared. As you check each ticket, it will be stamped as either a WINNER or a LOSER. If the ticket is a winner, your bankroll will immediately be credited. As in a real casino, you must claim your winning tickets.

Note that you cannot collect on won tickets that were previously played unless you actually check the tickets by opening up the keno game and using the directional arrows to display them. If the ticket is a winner, it will immediately be displayed and the winnings will get credited to your bankroll.

Clicking on the left arrow, where it says BACKWARDS, takes

the top ticket and places it on the bottom of the stack so that the ticket below is revealed; clicking on the right arrow, where it says FORWARD, does the reverse - it takes the bottom ticket and places it on top of the stack. Clicking repeatedly scrolls tickets in their respective order. Each ticket played will have the game # recorded in the middle of the ticket next to "VALID ON GAMES."

Going backward or forward with the directional arrows will show you only the tickets you actually played. To see the numbers that were drawn for that game, match up the game # by using the directional arrows in the GAME HISTORY display. For example, if you played a ticket in game # 04473 last week, you can use the directional arrows in both displays to show your actual ticket and the numbers drawn.

You may store the last 100 tickets played even though each ticket may have played 20 games each. When the 100 ticket limit is reached, the game will alert you that you've reached your limit and you'll need to trash old tickets to make new ones.

THE REPLAY TICKET BUTTON

Clicking on the REPLAY TICKET button will replay the current ticket shown for the following game, whether that ticket was played the previous game, or any number of games ago. For example, if you had played a five spot ticket 10 games ago with the numbers 17, 64, 65, 66 and 80, and scrolled on the backward arrow until that ticket was displayed, you would simply hit REPLAY TICKET to play the same ticket again on the upcoming game.

THE TRASH TICKET BUTTON

This button allows you to discard old tickets so you can make room for new ones when you've reached the 100 ticket limit. You can use the directional arrows to go to the ticket you wish to discard, whether it's one you played 90 tickets ago, or the current one you've marked up and which you're unhappy with. Hitting TRASH TICKET will discard the ticket currently on display to the left of your screen.

41

ROULETTE INSTRUCTIONS

QUICK PLAY INSTRUCTIONS

1. Set BET UNIT by clicking on numbered bet keys.
2. Click on any or all of the bet spots on the table to place your wagers.
3. Press SPIN on the bottom right of screen. The dealer will spin the wheel.

Roulette Button Bar

HOW TO MAKE A BET

You must first set a BET UNIT amount to make bets. Once a bet amount is entered in the BET UNIT area, you place bets by clicking on any of the available bets at the roulette table.

REMOVING BETS

Any bet on the layout may be removed at any time prior to the spin of the wheel.

AVAILABLE BETS

You have a choice of over 150 possible bets at roulette and they are placed in the same locations in this game as in a standard casino. There are single number, two number, three number, four number, five number, six number, column, dozens and even-money bets at your disposal.

For information on all these bets and where they get placed, read the roulette *Gaming and Strategy Section* (pages 128-144) or consult the on-line help for roulette. You can also use the message bar area for assistance on where to place bets by moving the cursor *slowly* over the layout. Available bets and their payouts will be indicated when the cursor is positioned on an area where such a bet is allowed. Click there and your bet will be placed.

HOW TO SPIN THE WHEEL

Once a bet has been placed on the table, the SPIN button to the far right of the table becomes active. When you are finished placing all your bets, click on this button to spin the wheel and get the action going. Bets may not be placed once the SPIN button is clicked.

All bets will be paid off or collected after each spin. When the payoffs are completed, the dealer will be ready to accept your new bets and get the action going again.

THE NUMBERS BOARD

The game keeps track of the last six winning numbers on the NUMBERS BOARD located on the upper left hand of your screen. This feature helps keeping track of the mini-trends so important to short systems players.

For full *longer-history* tracking, and as the serious players do and have done for centuries, you would want to write down winning numbers with paper and pen. Keeping track of previous winning numbers is at the heart of all roulette systems.

MESSAGE BAR

As the cursor is moved over the roulette layout, the message bar will display the bet that you can make by clicking on the spot and the payoffs for that bet.

SLOTS INSTRUCTIONS

Slots Button Bar

INTRODUCTION

You have a choice of 40 slots machines to try your luck. Some pay better than others; in fact, there are a couple of machines that will pay more than any machine you'll find in Las Vegas. But we're not telling you which ones!

HOW TO PLAY THE SLOTS

To bet the full five coins, press BET MAX and the reels will automatically be spun. You may also bet 1 or 2 coins on a three coin machine, and 1, 2, 3 or 4 coins on a five coin machine, by pressing BET ONE for each coin you want bet.

The number of coins played will register in the COINS PLAYED display on the bottom right of the machine. Then press SPIN. If you happen to press BET ONE enough times for the maximum number of coins, the reels will be spun.

CREDITS AND WINNER PAID

The area marked WINNER PAID shows the amount won on the current spin, while CREDITS lists the total current amount of credits you've earned through wins. Thus, after a win, you may see "25" in the WINNER PAID area (representing a new 25 unit win) and "75" in the CREDITS display .

If you press BET MAX, WINNER PAID will reset to 0 for the new game being played and three coins will be deducted from your CREDIT, which in this example, will now show "72."

Winning spins will get credited in the area marked CREDITS and remain there until you either exit the game, cash out (see CASH OUT button below), or run out of credits. New bets are always financed from the credits unless there are no credits remaining. In that case, bets will be deducted directly from your bankroll.

HITTING THE JACKPOT! - EXITING THE ANIMATION

If you hit the jackpot and tire of watching the long payout animation, *right* clicking on your mouse or hitting the space bar will exit the animation, credit you with the full total and return you to the normal mode.

CASH OUT BUTTON

The CASH OUT button plays no functional role in our game, but is a fun way for you to watch your winnings drop into the hold. You may click the CASH OUT button whenever there are earnings accumulated in the CREDITS display. If your payout happens to be long and you want to exit the animation, *right click* on your mouse, or click the space bar, to return you to the normal mode.

When you're finished playing, you can exit the game (by going to another game or exiting the program altogether), or you can CASH OUT. Either way, all credits you've earned will automatically be credited toward your bankroll.

PLAYING ON CREDITS

Serious slots and video poker players like to play on credits and use their starting credit total as a measuring stick for the progress of their play. We have given you three options: ADD 50 CREDITS, ADD 100 CREDITS, and ADD 200 CREDITS, all of which are found under the OPTIONS menu. Clicking this option loads your credits to the chosen amount and of course, gets deducted directly from your bankroll.

VIDEO POKER INSTRUCTIONS

QUICK PLAY INSTRUCTIONS

1. Click on BET ONE to bet one coin, then press DEAL; or click on BET MAX to bet five coins, and five cards will automatically be dealt.

2. Keep cards by clicking on cards themselves ("HELD" will appear) or reclick to discard that decision.

3. Click DRAW on bottom right of screen. New cards will replace those not marked HELD. This is your final hand.

4. Winning hands will get credited in the CREDITS display.

Video Poker Button Bar

HOW TO MAKE A BET

To bet the full five coins, press BET MAX and the cards will automatically be dealt. You may also bet 1, 2, 3 or 4 coins, by pressing BET ONE for each coin you want bet. The payout display above will light up for each coin played. Then press DEAL. If you press BET ONE five times, cards will automatically be dealt.

HOW TO PLAY A HAND

Once the cards have been dealt, you may choose to keep any or all of the cards by clicking on them. A HELD will appear beneath the cards clicked. You may remove that HELD by reclicking on the card. After you've made your decision, click DRAW, and new cards will be dealt. Your hand is now complete.

If you're dealt five cards you want to keep, for example a full house, remember to HOLD each card before pressing DRAW or your cards will be discarded!

CREDITS AND WINNER PAID

The area marked WINNER PAID shows the amount won on the

current spin, while CREDITS lists the total current amount of credits you've earned through wins. Thus, after a win, you may see "25" in the WINNER PAID area (representing this new 25 unit win) and "75" in the CREDITS display .

If you press BET MAX, WINNER PAID will reset to 0 for the new game being played and three coins will be deducted from your CREDIT, which in this example, will now show "70."

Winning spins will get credited in the area marked CREDITS and remain there until you either exit the game, cash out (see CASH OUT button below), or run out of credits. New bets are always financed from the credits unless there are no credits remaining. In that case, bets will be deducted directly from your bankroll.

HITTING THE JACKPOT! - EXITING THE ANIMATION

If you hit the big jackpot and want to exit the payout animation, *right* clicking on your mouse or hitting the space bar will exit the animation while crediting you with the full jackpot total.

CASH OUT BUTTON

The CASH OUT button plays no functional role in our game, but is a fun way for you to watch your winnings drop into the hold. You may click the CASH OUT button whenever there are earnings accumulated in the CREDITS display. If your payout happens to be long and you want to exit the animation, *right click* on your mouse, or click the space bar, to return you to the normal mode.

When you're finished playing, you can exit the game (by going to another game or exiting the program altogether), or you can CASH OUT. Either way, all credits you've earned will automatically be credited toward your bankroll.

PLAYING ON CREDITS

Serious video poker players like to play on credits and use their starting credit total as a measuring stick for their winnings. You have three options: ADD 50 CREDITS, ADD 100 CREDITS, and ADD 200 CREDITS, all of which are found under the OPTIONS menu. Clicking this option loads your credits to the chosen amount.

47

GAMING & STRATEGY
SECTION

PLAYING BLACKJACK TO WIN

INTRODUCTION

Blackjack turned into the most popular casino game when the word got out - that it can be beaten! With proper play, you can actually have the edge over the casino, and thus, the expectation to win money every time you play.

We cover the fundamentals of casino blackjack here - the rules of the game, the players' options, the variations offered in casinos, how to bet, casino jargon, how to play and everything else you'll need to know about playing winning casino blackjack.

We'll also show you a very effective card counting method, so that you can really go for the winning sessions.

BEGINNER'S GUIDE TO CASINO BLACKJACK

Object of the Game

The player's object in casino blackjack is to beat the dealer. This can be achieved in two ways:

1 - When the player has a higher total than the dealer without exceeding 21.

2 - When the dealer's total exceeds 21 (assuming the player has not exceeded 21 first).

If the player and the dealer both hold the same total of 21 or less, the hand is a **push**, a tie, nobody wins.

Busting or Breaking - Automatic Losers

If the drawing of additional cards to the initial two cards dealt causes the point total to exceed 21, then that hand is said to be **busted**, an automatic loss. Busted hands should be turned up immediately. Once the player has busted, his hand is lost, even if the dealer busts as well afterwards. If the dealer busts, all remaining players automatically win their bets.

Blackjack - Automatic Winner

If the original two card hand contains an Ace with any 10 or face card (J,Q,K), the hand is called a **blackjack**, or **natural**, and is an automatic winner for the player whose bet is paid of at 3 to 2. If the dealer gets a blackjack, all players lose their bets. (The dealer wins only the player's bet, not the 3 to 2 payoff the player receives for a blackjack.)

If both the dealer and the player are dealt a blackjack, the hand is a push. Blackjacks should be turned up immediately.

Payoffs

All bets are paid off at even money ($5 bet wins $5), except in cases where the player receives a blackjack which is a 3 to 2 payoff ($5 bet wins $7.50) or when the player exercises an option that allows him to double his bet. In these instances (doubling and splitting), the payoff is equal to the new doubled bet. If a bet is doubled from $5 to $10, a win would pay off $10.

Card Values

Each card is counted at face value. 2=2 points, 3=3 points, 10=10 points, while the face cards, Jack, Queen and King, are counted as 10 points. The Ace can be counted as 1 point or 11 points at the player's discretion. When the Ace is counted as 11 points, that hand is called **soft**, as in the hand Ace, 7 = *soft 18*. All other totals, including hands where the Ace counts as 1 point, are called hard, as in the hand 10, 6, A = *hard 17*.

The dealer must count his Ace as 11 if that gives him a hand totaling 17 to 21, otherwise he must count the Ace as 1 point.

In some casinos the rules dictate that the dealer must draw on soft 17. In these casinos, the dealer's Ace will count as 1 point when combined with cards totalling 6 points, and the dealer will have to draw until he forms a hand of at least hard 17.

Single vs. Multiple Deck Basics

In a single or or double deck game, the player is dealt his cards face down and gets to physically hold them.

In a game of four or more decks the cards will be dealt out of a shoe (as opposed to hand-held as in the one or two deck games), and the player is not supposed to touch them at any time. Instead, playing decisions are indicated by hand signals.

Dealer's Rules

The dealer must play by prescribed guidelines. He must draw to any hand 16 or below and stand on any total 17-21. As mentioned above, some casinos require the dealer to draw on soft 17. The dealer has no options and cannot deviate from these rules.

PLAYER'S OPTIONS

Unlike the dealer, the player can vary his strategy. After receiving his first two cards the player has the following options:

Drawing (Hitting)

If the player is not satisfied with his two card total he can draw additional cards. To draw a card, the player scrapes the felt surface with his cards, scraping toward his body. In a game where both the player's cards are dealt face up, the player is not supposed to touch the cards and instead scratches the felt with his index finger or points toward the cards if he desires additional cards.

Standing

When a player is satisfied with his original two card total, and does not wish to draw additional cards, he signals this by sliding his cards face down under his bet. When the cards are dealt face up, the player indicates his decision to stand pat by waving is hand palm down over his cards.

Doubling Down

This option allows the player to double his original bet, in which case he must draw one additional card to his hand and cannot draw any additional cards thereafter. To double down, the player turns his cards face up, and places them in front of his bet. Then he takes an amount equal to his original bet and places those chips next to that bet, so that there are now two equivalent bets side by side. In games where the cards are dealt face up, the player simply places the additional bet next to his original to indicate the double down.

The dealer will then deal one card face down, usually slipping that card under the player's bet. The bettor may look at that card if he desires.

Splitting Pairs

If dealt a pair of identical value cards, such as 3-3, 7-7, 8-8 (any combination of 10, J, Q, K is considered a pair), the player can split these cards so that two separate hands are formed. To split a pair, the player turns the pair face up, separates them, putting each card in its own place in front of his bet. He then places a bet equal to the original wager behind the second hand. Each hand is played separately, using finger and hand signals to indicate hitting and standing.

In games where both player cards are dealt face up, the split is indicated by placing the additional bet next to the original one, and after, using hand signals as above to indicate hitting or standing.

If the first card dealt to either split hand has a value identical to the original split cards, that card may be split again (resplit) into a third hand, with the exception of Aces. When the player splits Aces, he can receive only one card on each Ace and may not draw again, no matter what card is drawn.

Doubling Down After Splitting

The player can double down on one or both of the hands resulting from a split according to the normal doubling rules of the casino. This option is offered in all Atlantic City casinos and in certain Nevada casinos.

For example, if a pair of 8s are split, and a 3 is drawn to the first 8 for an 11, the player may elect to double down on that 11.

He does so by placing an amount equal to the original bet next to the 11, and receives only one additional card for that hand. The other 8 is played separately and can be doubled as well should an advantageous card such as a 2 or 3 be drawn.

Since options allowed are often in flux, sometimes changing from one month to the next, when playing, check to see if this advantageous option is available.

Surrender (Late Surrender)

The player may "surrender" his original two card hand and forfeit one half of his bet after it has been determined that the dealer does not have a blackjack and before the player has exercised any of his other options. Surrender is offered in only a few casinos.

To surrender, the bettor turns both his cards face up, puts them above his bet, and says "surrender," or in a game where both player cards are dealt face up, he announces his intention verbally to the dealer. The dealer will collect the cards and take one half of the bet.

Insurance

If the dealer shows an Ace as his upcard, he will ask the players if they want insurance. If any player exercises this option, he is in effect betting that the dealer has a 10-value card as his hole card, a blackjack. To take insurance, the player places up to one-half the amount of his bet in the area marked "insurance."

If the dealer does indeed have a blackjack, he gets paid 2 to 1 on the insurance bet, while losing the original bet. In effect, the transaction is a "standoff," and no money is lost. If the dealer does not have a blackjack, the insurance bet is lost and play continues.

If the player holds a blackjack and takes insurance on the dealer's Ace, the payoff will be even-money whether the dealer has a blackjack or not. Suppose the player has a $10 bet and takes insurance for $5 on his blackjack. If the dealer has a blackjack, the player wins 2 to 1 on his $5 insurance bet and ties with his own blackjack. If the dealer doesn't have a blackjack, the player loses the $5 insurance bet but gets paid 3 to 2 on his blackjack. Either way the bettor wins $10.

Insurance Strategy

Insurance is a bad bet for the following reason: Making an insurance wager is betting that the dealer has a 10 under his Ace. Since the insurance payoff is 2 to 1, the wager will only be a profitable option for the player when the ratio of 10s to other cards is either equal to or less than 2 to 1.

A full deck has 36 non-tens and 16 tens, a ratio greater than 2 to 1. If the first deal off the top of the deck gives us a hand of 9,7, and the dealer shows an Ace, then we know three cards, all non-tens. Now the ratio is 33 to 16, still greater than 2 to 1, still a poor bet. If you have two 10s for a 20, then the ratio is 35 to 14, an even worse bet.

In a multiple deck game, taking insurance is even a worse bet than in a single deck one.

Insuring a Blackjack

Taking insurance when you have a blackjack is also a bad bet, despite the well-intentioned advice of dealers and other players to "always insure a blackjack." When you have a blackjack, you know three cards, your 10 and Ace, and the dealer's Ace. The already poor starting ratio of 36 tens to 16 non-tens gets worse, becoming 34 to 15 in a single deck game.

Taking insurance when you have a blackjack gives the house an 8% advantage, a poor proposition for the player.

The Play of the Game

The dealer begins by shuffling the cards and offering the cut to one of the players. If refused, it is offered to another player. The dealer then completes the cut, and removes the top card, called the **burn card**.

In single and double deck games, the burn card is either put under the deck face up, where all subsequent cards will be placed, or is put face down into a plastic case (procedures vary from casino to casino) to be followed similarly by future discards.

In games dealt out of a shoe, the burn card will be placed most of the way into the shoe and discards will be put in the plastic case.

Players must make their bets before the cards are dealt.

The dealer deals clockwise from his left to his right, one card at a time, until each player and the dealer have received two cards. The players cards are usually dealt face down in a single or double deck game, though it makes no difference if they are dealt face up as they usually are in a game dealt out of a shoe, for the dealer is bound by strict rules from which he cannot deviate.

The dealer deals only one of his two cards face up. This card is called an **upcard**. The face down card is known as the **hole card** or the **downcard**.

If the dealer's upcard is an Ace, he will ask the players if they want insurance. Players that decide to take that option may bet up to one-half their wager in front of their bet in the area marked insurance.

If the dealer has a blackjack, all players that did not take insurance lose their original bets. Players that took insurance break even on the play. It is an automatic winner for the house. If the dealer doesn't have a blackjack, he collects the lost insurance bets and play continues.

Play begins with the bettor on the dealer's left, in the position known as **first base**.

This player has the option to stand, hit, double down, split (if he has two cards of equal value) or surrender (if allowed). A player may draw cards until he is satisfied with his total or busts, or he may exercise one of the other options discussed above.

Play then moves to the next player. If any player busts (goes over 21) or receives a blackjack, he must turn over his cards immediately. If a bust, the dealer will collect the lost bet. If a blackjack, the dealer will pay the player 3 to 2 on his bet.

After the last player has acted upon his cards, the dealer will turn his hole card over so that all players can view both of his cards. He must play his hand according to the strict guidelines regulating his play; drawing to 17, then standing. (In some casinos the dealer must draw to a soft 17.) If the dealer busts, all players still in the game for that round of play win automatically.

After playing his hand, the dealer will turn over each player's cards in turn, paying the winners, and collecting from the losers. Once the bettor has played his hand, he shouldn't touch his cards again. He should let the dealer expose his hand which he will do when he has played out his own hand.

In a game dealt from a shoe (four or more decks), the player should never touch the cards anyway.

When the round has been completed, all players must place a new bet before the next deal.

Casino Personnel

The casino employee responsible for the running of the blackjack game is called the **dealer**. The dealer's duties are to deal the cards to the players, and play out his own hand according to the rules of the game. He converts money into chips for players entering the game or buying in for more chips during the course of the game, makes the correct payoffs for winning hands, and collects bets from the losers.

The dealer's supervisor - technically called the **floorman**, but more commonly referred to as the **pit boss** - is responsible for the supervision of between 4-6 tables. He makes sure the games are run smoothly and he settles any disputes that may arise with a player. More importantly, his job is to oversee the exchange of money and to correct any errors that may occur.

Entering a Game

To enter a blackjack game, sit down at any unoccupied seat at the blackjack table, place the money you wish to gamble with near the betting box in front of you and inform the dealer that you would like to get some chips for your cash. Chips may be purchased in various denominations. Let the dealer know which chips or combination of chips you'd like.

The dealer will take your money and call out the amount he is changing so that the pit boss is aware that a transaction is taking place and can supervise that exchange.

Tipping

The best way to tip a dealer is to place a bet for the dealer in front of your own bet, so that his chances of winning that toke are tied up with your hand. If the hand is won, you both win together; if the hand is lost, you lose together.

By being partners on the hand, you establish camaraderie with the dealer. Naturally, he or she will be rooting for you to win. This is the best way to tip, for when you win, the dealer wins double - the tip amount you bet plus the winnings from that bet.

The Decks of Cards

Nevada casinos use one, two, four, six and sometimes as many as eight decks of cards in their blackjack games. Often, within the same casino, single and multiple deck games will be offered.

Typically though, outside of Nevada, multiple deck blackjack dealt out of a shoe is the standard of play in the world whether played in Atlantic City, on casino boats, in Indian casinos or anywhere else blackjack may be found.

When one or two decks are used, the dealer holds the cards in his hand. When more than two decks are used, the cards are dealt from a rectangular plastic or wooden device known as a **shoe**. The shoe is designed to hold multiple decks of cards, and allows the cards to be easily removed one at a time by the dealer.

Each deck used in blackjack is a standard pack of 52 cards, consisting of 4 cards of each value, Ace through King. Suits have no relevance in blackjack. Only the numerical value of the cards count.

RULES & VARIATIONS OF THE CASINO CENTERS

Blackjack games are basically the same wherever played, though the rules and variations vary from casino center to casino center, and sometimes, they even differ within a casino itself.

However, the strategies we'll show you will arm you for any game, and give you the tools to be a winner no matter the variation.

The standard casino game is the same no matter where you play blackjack. Following are the main changes you'll find from one game to another, all of them being relatively minor. The first condition favors the player, the second, the house.

• Dealer stands on all 17s vs. dealer hits on soft 17

• Single deck vs. multiple deck (two, four, six or eight decks)

• Doubling down on any initial two card combination vs. doubling down restricted to certain totals, 10 and 11 only, for example)

• Doubling after splitting allowed vs. not allowed

Nevada Rules

The Las Vegas Strip rules are advantageous to the player and gives one a slight edge on the single deck game if our strategies are followed. The rule exceptions noted in Downtown Las Vegas and in Northern Nevada games are slightly disadvantageous to the player, but these can easily be overcome by using the winning techniques presented later.

Las Vegas Strip Rules

• Dealer must draw on all totals of 16 or less, and stand on all totals of 17-21.

• Player may take insurance on a dealer's Ace.

• Insurance payoffs are 2 to 1.

• Player receives a 3 to 2 payoff on his blackjack.

• Player may double down on any initial two card combination.

• Identical pairs may be split, resplit, and drawn to as desired with the exception of split Aces, on which the player is allowed only one hit on each Ace.

• One, two, four and bigger deck games are standard.

Downtown Las Vegas Rules

Rules and condition are the same as the Las Vegas Strip rules with one exception:

- Dealer must draw to soft 17.

Northern Nevada Rules

Same as Las Vegas Strip rules with two exceptions:

- Dealer must draw to soft 17.
- Doubling is restricted to two card totals of 10 and 11 only.

Atlantic City Rules

To protect against collusion between the player and the dealer, the dealer does not check his hole card for a blackjack (as is standard in Nevada) until all players have finished playing out their hands. This safeguard does not affect the player's chances of winning, for if the dealer does indeed have a blackjack, any additional money the player may have wagered on a doubled or split hand will be returned. Only the original bet is lost.

The standard Atlantic City rules are:

- Dealer must draw to all totals 16 or less, and stand on all totals of 17-21.
- Player may take insurance on a dealer's Ace.
- Insurance payoffs are 2 to 1.
- Player receives a 3 to 2 payoff on his blackjack.
- Player may double on any initial two card combination.
- Identical pairs may be split but not resplit.
- Doubling after splitting allowed.
- Four, six and eight decks are standard.

Blackjack in Other Locales

No longer is legalized casino gambling in North America restricted to just Nevada and Atlantic City. Now players may take on casinos in Indian reservations, riverboats, and in Canada. Blackjack rules in these venues will be similar to the Atlantic City or Nevada versions, and a player following the strategies we'll show will be prepared to win wherever the game may be played.

THE OPTIMAL BASIC STRATEGIES

The Ten Factor

The most striking feature of blackjack is the dominant role that the 10 value cards (10, J, Q, K) play - what we call the **ten factor**. Collectively, the 10s constitute just under 1/3 of the deck (16 out of 52 cards). Because 10s are such a dominant factor in a deck of cards, it's correct to think of the dealer's hand as *gravitating* toward a total 10 points greater than his exposed upcard.

Thus, for example, starting out with an upcard of 9, the dealer will make a hand of 19 about 36% of the time and 19 or better 52% of the time.

The Dealer Rules and the Ten Factor

Our strategy is based on the fact that the dealer must play by prescribed guidelines from which he cannot deviate. He must draw to all totals 16 or below, and stand on all totals 17-21 (except in casinos that require the dealer to draw to soft 17). All hard totals that exceed hard 21 are automatic dealer losses.

Our knowledge of the 10 factor and the dealer's rules allows us to separate the dealer's upcards into two distinct groupings: 2s through 6s, the dealer *stiff cards*, and 7s through As (Aces), the dealer *pat cards*.

We'll base our strategies accordingly.

The high concentration of 10 value cards in the deck tells us that the dealer has a good chance of busting when his upcard is a 2, 3, 4, 5 or 6, a *stiff card*, and that there is an excellent chance he will make his hand when showing the *pat cards*, the 7, 8, 9, 10, A. Even when he hasn't a 10 in the hole, combinations such as 89; A7; 99 and so forth, give him an automatic pat hand as well.

General Principles

1. When the dealer shows a 7, 8, 9, 10 or A, hit all hard totals of 16 or below (unless doubling or splitting is more profitable - in any case, you will always draw a card).

2. When the dealer shows a 2, 3, 4, 5 or 6, stand on all hard totals of 12 or more. Do not bust against a dealer stiff card. Exception - Hit 12 vs. 2, 3.

Player Hand of 11 or Less - (Hard Totals)

Always draw to any hard total 11 or less (unless a doubling or splitting option is more profitable). There is no risk of busting, no matter what is drawn, while the drawing of a card can only strengthen our hand.

Player Hand of 17-21 - (Hard Totals)

Always stand on these hard totals (17-21), for the risk of busting is too high to make drawing worthwhile.

Player Hand of 12-16 - (Hard Totals)

With these hands, our play is not an obvious draw such as the 11 or less grouping for the risk of drawing a 10 or other high card and busting is substantial. Our hand is not an obvious stand decision either such as the 17-21 grouping, for the only times we will win with these weak totals of 12-16 are the times that the dealer busts.

It is when we hold hard totals 12-16 (stiffs) that the player's big disadvantage of having to go first (the only built-in house advantage) is a costly proposition. If we draw to hard totals and bust, we are automatic losers. But, on the other hand, if we stand, we will win with these weak totals only when the dealer busts.

It is important to realize that the decision to hit or stand with hard totals 12-16 is a strategy of minimizing losses, for no matter what we do, we have a potentially losing hand against any dealer upcard. Do not expect to win when you hold a stiff.

However, in order to maximize the gain from our overall strategy, we must minimize the losses in disadvantageous situations (as above), and maximize our gains in advantageous ones.

Player Totals of 12-16 vs. Dealer Pat Cards 7 - A

When the dealer's upcard is a 7 through an Ace, you should expect the dealer to make his hand, for he will bust only about one time in four, a mere 25% of the time. If we stand on our hard totals 12-16, we will win only the times that the dealer busts.

You will bust often when drawing to your stiffs, but do not let that dissuade you form hitting your stiffs against pat cards. The strategy on these plays is to minimize losses. We cannot afford to stand and sacrifice our bet to the 3 out of 4 hands that the dealer will make.

When the dealer shows a 7, 8, 9, 10, or Ace, hit all hard totals 16 or below.

Player Totals of 12-16 vs. Dealer Pat Cards 2 - 6

The greater busting potential of the dealer stiff cards makes standing with hard player totals of 12-16 a big gain over drawing. While we will win only 40% of these hands (the times that the dealer busts), standing is a far superior strategy to drawing, for we will bust too often drawing to our own stiffs against upcards that will bust fairly often themselves.

The times that we would make pat totals by drawing wouldn't guarantee us winners either, for the dealer will often make equal or better totals.

On these plays, our disadvantage of having to go first makes drawing too costly, for once we bust, we automatically lose. Though the dealer will make more hands than bust, our strategy here is to minimize losses so that when we get our good hands, we'll come out an overall winner.

Exception - Hit Player 12 vs. 2, 3 - This is the only basic strategy exception to drawing with a stiff total against a dealer's stiff upcard. The double bust factor is not as costly on these plays, for only the 10s will bust our 12. Similarly, the dealer will bust less often showing a 2 or 3 than with the other stiff cards, 4, 5, 6.

HITTING AND STANDING - SOFT TOTALS
Player Hand of A2, A3, A4, A5

Unless the player is able to double down, he should always draw a card to these hands. Standing is a poor option, for these totals will win only when the dealer busts. The player has nothing to lose by drawing (no draw can bust these totals), and may improve his total. Players that stand on these hands might just as well give the casinos their money.

Draw on A2-A5 against all dealer upcards.

For soft totals A6 - A9, we want to know:

1- What are our chances of winning by standing?

2- What are the chances of improving our hand by drawing additional cards?

Player Hand of Soft 17 (A6)

Always draw on soft 17 no matter what the dealer shows as an upcard. (In Las Vegas and Atlantic City and other locations where allowed, the correct strategy may be to double down. See doubling section.) This standing total is so weak that attempting to improve our hand by drawing is always a tremendous gain against any upcard.

When a casino requires the dealer to draw to soft 17, it is a disadvantageous rule to the player. Though the dealer will sometimes bust by drawing to a soft 17, in the long run he will make more powerful totals and have more winners. It affects the player the same way.

Player Hand of Soft 18

Against dealer stiff totals of 2, 3, 4, 5 and 6, standing with our 18 is a smart strategy move (unless playing Las Vegas or Atlantic City doubling rules where doubling will often be a big player gain). We have a strong total against these weak dealer upcards.

Stand against dealer upcards of 7 and 8, for our 18 is a solid hand. Against the 7, we have a winning total, and against the 8, we figure to have a potential push, as these dealer upcards gravitate toward 17 and 18 respectively. We do not want to risk our strong position by drawing.

Against the powerful dealer upcards of 9, 10, Ace, our standing total of 18 is a potentially losing hand and thus we try to improve it. Soft 18 is only a fair total and by drawing we are not chancing a powerful total but rather attempting to improve a weak situation.

As a matter of fact, for every 100 plays (at $1 a play) that we draw rather than stand on soft 18 vs. 9 and 10, we will gain $9 and $4 respectively. You must realize that 18 vs. 9, 10, Ace is not a winning hand and since our 18 is a soft total, we have a chance to minimize losses by drawing.

Player Hand of Soft 19 and 20

These hands are strong player totals as they stand. Do not draw any cards. We have no need of improving these already powerful totals.

DOUBLING DOWN

Doubling down is valuable option for it gives the player a chance to double his bet in advantageous situations.

One of the most important factors to consider when contemplating the doubling option is the 10 factor - we are more likely to draw a 10 on our double than any other card value. Thus, doubling on a total of 11, where the drawing of a 10 gives us an unbeatable 21, is a more powerful double than an initial two card total of 9, where the drawing of 10 gives us a strong total of 19, not as powerful as the 21.

On the other hand, we would not double any hand of hard 12 or more, for the drawing of a 10 would bust our total, and we would have an automatic loser at double the bet.

The 10 factor is also an important strategic consideration, for it affects the dealer's busting potential. We double more aggressively against the weakest of the dealer stiff cards, the 4, 5 and 6, and less aggressively against the other stiff cards, the 2 and 3.

The only times we will double against the dealer pat cards are when our doubling totals of 10 and 11, hands that could turn into 20s and 21s, are powerful themselves.

Multiple Deck Doubling Strategy

You'll notice that the doubling strategies for multiple deck play are somewhat less aggressive than the single deck game, a difference we'll discuss a little later on.

Where multiple deck strategies differ from the single deck, an asterisk will denote the strategy change, and that change will be indicated.

Doubling 11 *

This is the strongest doubling hand for the player and should be doubled against all the dealer upcards in a single deck game. If we draw a 10 value card on our double, we will have a 21, the strongest hand we can have. At best, the dealer can tie us.

*Do not double 11 vs. Ace in multiple deck games.

Doubling 10

This is the second strongest doubling hand for the player and should be doubled against the dealer's 2 through 9. Our hard 10 gravitates toward a 20, an overwhelmingly strong hand against these dealer upcards.

Doubling 9 *

Double 9 against 2 through 6 only*. The high busting potential of the dealer stiff cards (2-6) makes the 9 a profitable double down. We cannot double down against any of the pat cards (7-Ace) for our win potential when we do draw the 10 (for a total of 19) is not strong enough to compensate for the times when we draw a poor card and cannot draw again.

*Do not double 9 vs. 2 in a multiple deck game.

Doubling 8

Doubling 8 vs. 5, 6 is a valid play in a single deck game*. Our 8 gravitates toward an 18, only a fair total. However, the very high busting potential of the dealer 5 and 6 make this double a slight gain. Our 8 is not strong enough to make doubling against the other dealer upcards a good play.

* Do not double 8 vs. any upcard in a multiple deck game.

Doubling Down - Soft Totals

The high concentration of 10s play a different role in soft doubling than in hard doubling, for instead of having a positive effect on our chances of making a good total, the drawing of 10 will not even give us a pat hand on many of these doubles.

Doubling with soft totals is generally a gain against weak dealer upcards. The 10 factor figures strongly in the dealer's chances of busting, while on the other hand, the drawing of small and medium cards will often improve our hand to competitive and winning totals.

Doubling A2, A3, A4, A5 *

Double A2, A3, A4 and A5 against the dealer's 4, 5 and 6.

The very high busting probabilities of the dealer's 4, 5 and 6 makes doubling with our A2 to A5 profitable for the player. Again, the drawing of a 10 value card does not help our total, but the high dealer busting factor gives us an edge.

We do not double against the 2 and 3, because the dealer will make just too many hands with these upcards. The same is more strikingly true with the dealer pat cards, 7 through Ace.

* Do not double A2 or A3 vs. 4 in a multiple deck game.

Doubling A6 *

Double A6 vs. dealer 2, 3, 4, 5 and 6. The A6 is a more powerful double than the A2-A5, for the drawing of a 10 to the A6 will at least give us a pat total and a potential push against a dealer's 17. This "push" factor enables us to gain by doubling against the dealer's 2 and 3 despite the fact that the dealer will make more pat totals than with the weaker upcards 4, 5 and 6.

* Do not double A6 vs. 2 in a multiple deck game.

Doubling A7

Double A7 vs. 3, 4, 5 and 6. Our soft 18 is only a fair total and drawing an additional card won't risk the destruction of a powerful total such as a 19 or 20.

Soft 18 is a strong double against the weaker dealer stiffs 4, 5 and 6, but differs from the soft 17 in that we do not double against the 2. A standing total of 18 vs. a 2 is a stronger winning hand and we do not want to risk the weakening of this hand by doubling and having to draw a card.

Doubling A8, A9

We have two very strong totals here and do not want to risk our excellent chances of winning by attempting to double.

Stand with these powerful hands - do not double.

SPLITTING PAIRS

Splitting can do two valuable things. It can turn one poor total into two stronger hands, such as splitting a hard 16 (8-8) into two hands of 8 each, and it effectively doubles our bet.

The decision to split requires a closer look at our hand vs. the dealer's hand, for we must balance the standing total of our hand against the two proposed split hands to see if the split and result-ant doubling of our bet increases our expectation of winning.

Splitting Pairs - Multiple Deck

You'll notice that we'll split less aggressively against a mul-tiple deck game than against a single deck one. On the other hand, when the game offers doubling after splitting, we get more ag-gressive.

What happens when a multiple deck game offers doubling after splitting? We'll cover each of the possibilities in turn, show-ing you the best way to play no matter the situation.

Splitting 99

We will examine the decision to split 99 first, for it is a good example of the thinking process involved in splitting. First of all, we should note that this hand totaling 18 is only "fair," not a powerful total like a 19 or 20.

Splitting 9s - Dealer shows a 2, 3, 4, 5, 6

Split 99 against these dealer stiff cards. Our 18 is a winner, but splitting the hand into two halves of 9 each is a big gain. Each starting hand of 9, because of the 10 factor, gravitates toward strong player totals of 19.

The high busting potential of the dealer stiff cards gives us an excellent opportunity to maximize our gain in an advantageous situation.

Splitting 9s - Dealer shows a 7

Stand with 99 vs. dealer 7. We figure the dealer for a 17. Our standing total of 18 is a stronger total and a big potential winner. While splitting 9s will also produce a positive expectation of winning, the risking of our fairly secure 18 against the 7 for two strong but chancy totals reduces the gain.

We have the dealer beat. Stand.

Splitting 9s - Dealer shows an 8

Splitting 99 against the dealer's 8 is a big gain. Against the dealer's 8, we figure our 18 to be a potential push. However, by splitting the 18 into two hands of 9, we hope to turn our possible push into two potential winners. (Each 9 gravitates toward a total of 19, one point higher than the dealer's 18.)

Splitting 9s - Dealer shows a 9

Splitting 99 vs. the dealer's 9 is also a big gain. Against the 9, our 18 is a losing total, but splitting the 18 into two totals of 9 each reduces our potential loss. Rather than one losing total of 18, we have two potential pushes.

Splitting 9s - Dealer shows a 10 or Ace

Do not split 99 against the dealer's 10 or Ace. Our split hands of 9 gravitate toward good totals, but against these more powerful dealer upcards, splitting would be a poor play. We do not want to make one loser into two.

Splitting 22 and 33*

Split 22 vs. dealer 3-7.*   Split 33 vs. dealer 4 through 7*

The high busting probabilities of the dealer 4, 5 and 6 makes the 22 and 33 good splits. We split 22 vs. 3 and not 33 vs. 3, because of the lower player busting factor of our split hands of 2 each. The drawing of a 10 gives us another chance to improve on our 2, for correct basic strategy is to draw 12 vs. 3, while the drawing of a 10 on our 3 forces us to stand.

We do not split 22 or 33 vs. the dealer's 2, because the dealer's 2 does not bust often enough to make splitting a profitable play.

Splitting 22 and 33 vs. 7 seems unusual at first, for this play seems to exceed our normal strategic boundaries of making aggressive plays against the weak dealer stiff cards. Though the 7 is a pat card and will make a lot of pat hands, the 7 will also make the weakest totals, only gravitating toward a total of 17. Our starting totals of 2 and 3 will make hands of 18 or better about one-half the time.

Splitting 22 and 33 against the dealer's 7 will not make us money (because of the high busting factor of our hands), but they will produce a moderate gain over drawing to these hands.

Do not split 22 and 33 against the 8, 9, 10 or Ace. We do not want to make one loser into two losers.

*Multiple deck exception - Do not split 22 vs. 3.

**Games with doubling after splitting allowed (such as Atlantic City) - Split 22 and 33 vs. 2 through 7.

Splitting 44s**

Do not split 44 (unless doubling after splitting is allowed). The hard total of 8 gravitates toward a total of 18, a far better position than two weak starting totals of 4 each. Against the dealer stiff cards 2 through 6 we have a big gain by drawing to our 8. While drawing a 10 will not give us an overwhelmingly strong total, an 18 is far better than drawing the same 10 to a split 4.

We do not want to hold two weak hands of 4 each against the dealer pat cards, especially the dealer's 7 and 8, where we have a good starting total of 8.

**Games with doubling after splitting allowed (such as Atlantic City) - Split 44 vs. 5 and 6. The added possibilities of being able to double our bet should either or both of the split totals pull well makes this split an advantageous move.

Splitting 55

Never split 55. 55 by itself is an excellent starting total of 10. You do not want to break up this powerful player total into two terrible hands of 5 each. (Our 10 is an excellent doubling hand against dealer upcards of 2 through 9.)

Splitting 66*

Split 66 against dealer stiff cards 2 through 6 only*. Our hard total of 12 is not very favorable, nor are the split hands of 6 and 6 too promising either. We have a losing hand either way against all dealer upcards. However, we want to minimize our losses.

Against the dealer stiff cards 2, 3, 4, 5 and 6, our split hands of 6 and 6 will sometimes draw cards to give us pat totals of 17-21. Of course, we will often end up with stiff totals on the split pair (by the drawing of a 10 or other sufficiently large card) and be forced to stand. But the high dealer busting factor makes splitting 66 against the dealer stiffs a slight gain.

Obviously we will not split 66 against the dealer pat cards. We don't need two hands of 16 against a card that will bust only one time in four.

*Multiple deck exception - Do not split 66 vs. 2.

**Games with doubling after splitting allowed (such as Atlantic- City) - no exceptions. Split 66 vs. 2-6.

Splitting 77

Split 77 against dealer upcards of 2, 3, 4, 5, 6 and 7. Against the dealer stiff cards 2 through 6, two playable hands of 7 and 7 are preferable to one stiff total of 14. Splitting 77 is not a strong split, for these totals only gravitate toward a 17, but the high busting rate of the dealer stiff cards makes this split a big gain.

Splitting 77 against the dealer's 7 is also an excellent split, for we are taking one losing total of 14 into two potential pushes of 17 each.

We do not split 77 vs. the dealer's 8, 9, 10, Ace, for we do not want to take one poor total of 14 into two hands gravitating toward a second best total of only 17.

Splitting 88

Split 88 against all dealer upcards. Against the dealer's 2 through 8, we are taking one terrible hand of 16 into two playable totals of 8 each. There is a tremendous gain on all these plays.

Splitting 88 against the dealer's 9, 10, A are the strangest of the basic strategy plays. While splitting this 16 into two hands of 8 and 8 is not a winning situation against the strong dealer upcards of 9, 10 and A, it is an improvement over our very weak total of hard 16. Bear with this unusual play, for computer simulation studies have played out the hand millions of times for both drawing and splitting, and found that the player loses less by splitting 88. Realize that although the split is weak, it does produce a gain over drawing to our easily bustable 16.

Splitting 10,10

Do not split 10s. The hard total of 20 is a winning hand against all dealer upcards. Splitting 10s against any dealer upcard is a terrible play, for you are taking one "solid" winning hand into two good but uncertain wins.

Splitting AA

Split AA against all dealer upcards. Each Ace is a powerful starting total of 11 points. If we draw the 10, our 21 can't be beat. Splitting AA is a tremendous gain against all dealer upcards.

In all our charts on the following pages, the dealer's upcard is indicated by the horizontal number (running left to right) on the top row, and the player's hand is indicted by the vertical numbers (up and down) in the left column. The letters in the matrix indicate the correct strategy play.

Single Deck Master Chart

	2	3	4	5	6	7	8	9	10	A
7/less	H	H	H	H	H	H	H	H	H	H
62	H	H	H	H	H	H	H	H	H	H
44/53	H	H	H	D	D	H	H	H	H	H
9	D	D	D	D	D	H	H	H	H	H
10	D	D	D	D	D	D	D	D	H	H
11	D	D	D	D	D	D	D	D	D	D
12	H	H	S	S	S	H	H	H	H	H
13	S	S	S	S	S	H	H	H	H	H
14	S	S	S	S	S	H	H	H	H	H
15	S	S	S	S	S	H	H	H	H	H
16	S	S	S	S	S	H	H	H	H	H
A2	H	H	D	D	D	H	H	H	H	H
A3	H	H	D	D	D	H	H	H	H	H
A4	H	H	D	D	D	H	H	H	H	H
A5	H	H	D	D	D	H	H	H	H	H
A6	D	D	D	D	D	H	H	H	H	H
A7	S	D	D	D	D	S	S	H	H	H
A8	S	S	S	S	S	S	S	S	S	S
A9	S	S	S	S	S	S	S	S	S	S
22	H	spl	spl	spl	spl	spl	H	H	H	H
33	H	H	spl	spl	spl	spl	H	H	H	H
66	spl	spl	spl	spl	spl	H	H	H	H	H
77	spl	spl	spl	spl	spl	spl	H	H	H	H
88	spl	spl	spl	spl	spl	spl	spl	spl	spl	spl
99	spl	spl	spl	spl	spl	S	spl	spl	S	S
AA	spl	spl	spl	spl	spl	spl	spl	spl	spl	spl

H = Hit   **S** = Stand   **D** = Double   **spl** = Split
Do not split 44, 55 (double on 55) and 10s. Always split 88, AA

In Northern Nevada (or other places) where doubling down is restricted, usually to 10 and 11, hit instead of doubling on all hands where "D" is indicated, except on A7, where you should stand against the dealer's 3-6.

Single and Multiple Deck Blackjack Differences

As we have seen, the main variations in single and multiple deck strategy take place with our doubling and splitting options - moves which entail an increased wager on the hand.

The greater number of cards used in a multiple deck game makes the removal of any particular card or cards less significant compared to a single deck game, and as a result, our doubling and splitting strategies are less aggressive.

For example, the removal of three cards (5,3,5) creates a favorable imbalance for the player in a single deck game and makes a 53 double vs. the dealer's 5 a profitable play. The effective removal of these three cards gives the player a better chance of drawing a 10 on his 8 and, at the same time, increases the dealer's chance of busting. In a single deck game, 53 vs. 6 is a favorable double.

However, the removal of these three cards are barely felt in a multiple deck game, and thus, no favorable imbalance has been created and the double down is not a correct play.

This lack of sensitivity to particular card removal accounts for nine strategy changes in the multiple deck game from the preceding single deck master charts we just presented.

Except for the following nine changes in the doubling and splitting strategies, multiple deck basic strategy is identical to the single deck basic strategy.

In a multiple deck game:
- 1- Do not double hard 8 vs. 5; hit instead
- 2- Do not double hard 8 vs. 6; hit instead
- 3- Do not double hard 9 vs. 2; hit instead.
- 4.-Do not double hard 11 vs. Ace; hit instead.
- 5- Do not double A2 vs 4; hit instead.
- 6- Do not double A3 vs. 4; hit instead.
- 7- Do not double A6 vs 2; hit instead
- 8- Do not split 22 vs. 3; hit instead
- 9- Do not split 66 vs. 2; hit instead

Multiple Deck Master Chart

	2	3	4	5	6	7	8	9	10	A
7/less	H	H	H	H	H	H	H	H	H	H
8	H	H	H	H	H	H	H	H	H	H
9	H	D	D	D	D	H	H	H	H	H
10	D	D	D	D	D	D	D	D	H	H
11	D	D	D	D	D	D	D	D	D	H
12	H	H	S	S	S	H	H	H	H	H
13	S	S	S	S	S	H	H	H	H	H
14	S	S	S	S	S	H	H	H	H	H
15	S	S	S	S	S	H	H	H	H	H
16	S	S	S	S	S	H	H	H	H	H
A2	H	H	H	D	D	H	H	H	H	H
A3	H	H	H	D	D	H	H	H	H	H
A4	H	H	D	D	D	H	H	H	H	H
A5	H	H	D	D	D	H	H	H	H	H
A6	H	D	D	D	D	H	H	H	H	H
A7	S	D	D	D	D	S	S	H	H	H
A8	S	S	S	S	S	S	S	S	S	S
A9	S	S	S	S	S	S	S	S	S	S
22	H	H	spl	spl	spl	spl	H	H	H	H
33	H	H	spl	spl	spl	spl	H	H	H	H
66	H	spl	spl	spl	spl	H	H	H	H	H
77	spl	spl	spl	spl	spl	spl	H	H	H	H
88	spl	spl	spl	spl	spl	spl	spl	spl	spl	spl
99	spl	spl	spl	spl	spl	S	spl	spl	S	S
AA	spl	spl	spl	spl	spl	spl	spl	spl	spl	spl

H = Hit   **S** = Stand   **D** = Double   **spl** = Split
Do not split 44, 55 (double on 55) and 10s. Always split 88 and AA

In Northern Nevada (or other places) where doubling down is restricted, usually to 10 and 11, hit instead of doubling on all hands where "D" is indicated, except on A7, where you should stand against the dealer's 3-6.

Atlantic City Master Chart

	2	3	4	5	6	7	8	9	10	A
7/less	H	H	H	H	H	H	H	H	H	H
8	H	H	H	H	H	H	H	H	H	H
9	H	D	D	D	D	H	H	H	H	H
10	D	D	D	D	D	D	D	D	H	H
11	D	D	D	D	D	D	D	D	D	H
12	H	H	S	S	S	H	H	H	H	H
13	S	S	S	S	S	H	H	H	H	H
14	S	S	S	S	S	H	H	H	H	H
15	S	S	S	S	S	H	H	H	H	H
16	S	S	S	S	S	H	H	H	H	H
A2	H	H	H	D	D	H	H	H	H	H
A3	H	H	H	D	D	H	H	H	H	H
A4	H	H	D	D	D	H	H	H	H	H
A5	H	H	D	D	D	H	H	H	H	H
A6	H	D	D	D	D	H	H	H	H	H
A7	S	D	D	D	D	S	S	H	H	H
A8	S	S	S	S	S	S	S	S	S	S
A9	S	S	S	S	S	S	S	S	S	S
22	spl	spl	spl	spl	spl	spl	H	H	H	H
33	spl	spl	spl	spl	spl	spl	H	H	H	H
44	H	H	H	spl	spl	H	H	H	H	H
66	spl	spl	spl	spl	spl	H	H	H	H	H
77	spl	spl	spl	spl	spl	spl	H	H	H	H
88	spl	spl	spl	spl	spl	spl	spl	spl	spl	spl
99	spl	spl	spl	spl	spl	S	spl	spl	S	S
AA	spl	spl	spl	spl	spl	spl	spl	spl	spl	spl

H = Hit   **S** = Stand   **D** = Double   **spl** = Split

Do not split 55 and 10s. Always split 88 and AA.

PLAYER'S OPTIONS

Use these strategies where the following options are permitted:

Doubling Down Permitted After Splitting

This option allows the player to double down on one or more of the hands resulting from a split according to the standard doubling rules of the casino. When this doubling after splitting is allowed, we'll split more aggressively so that we may take advantage of good doubling situations that can arise as a consequence of the split. This option is favorable to the player.

Our Hand		Single Deck	Multiple Deck
22	split against	2-7	2-7
33	split against	2-7	2-7
44	split against	4-6	5-6
66	split against	2-7	2-6
77	split against	2-8	2-7

Late Surrender (Surrender)

A player option to forfeit his hand and lose half his bet after it has been determined that the dealer does not have a blackjack. This option is favorable to the player.

Our Hand		Single Deck	Multiple Deck
16*	surrender against	10, A	9,10, A
15	surrender against	10	10
77	surrender against	10	-

* Do not surrender 88 (split)

Early Surrender

A player option to forfeit his hand and lose half his bet *before* the dealer checks for a blackjack. A rare option, but extremely valuable for the player if available.

Dealer's Upcard		Player's Totals
A	early surrender with	5-7, 12-17
10	early surrender with	14-16
9	early surrender with	16*

Do not surrender soft totals   *Do not early surrender 88 (split)

76

CARD COUNTING STRATEGY

Computer studies have found that the proportionate removal of certain cards gives the player an advantage over the house, while the proportionate removal of others gives the house an advantage over the player.

Thus, as cards are removed from play, the player's chances of winning constantly change. Sometimes the depleted deck of cards will favor the house and sometimes the player. By learning to analyze a depleted deck of cards for favorability, and capitalizing on this situation by betting more when the remaining cards are in your favor, you can actually have an edge over the casino.

The heart of all winning systems at blackjack is based on this theory - betting more when you have the advantage, and less when the house has the advantage. This way, when you win, you win more, and when you lose, you lose less. Beginning with an even game (playing accurate basic strategy), this "maximize gain, minimize loss" betting strategy will give you an overall edge on the house.

How do we determine when we have the edge?

Computer studies have determined that 10s and Aces are the most valuable cards for the player, while the small cards, 2 through 7, are the most valuable cards for the house, 8s and 9s being relatively neutral. (The 2s and 7s are less important to the player than the 3s-6s, and as you'll see, we adjust for that in our count strategy.)

Off the top of the deck, with all cards still in play, the player has an even game with the house - neither side enjoys an advantage.* The odds shift in favor of the player when there is a higher ratio of 10s and As in the deck than normal, and shift in favor of the house when there is a higher ratio of small cards, 2s through 7s, than normal.

*Assuming the player plays perfect basic strategy as we've shown, and that the game is a single deck game with the favorable Las Vegas Strip rules. If the particular game has less liberal rules (Northern Nevada) or is a multiple deck game, the house enjoys a slight initial edge.

Winning With A Count Strategy

Knowledge of the proportion of 10 value cards (10s, Js, Qs and Ks) to small cards benefit the player for the simple reason that the player has the advantage of making judicious use of his options: drawing, standing, doubling down, splitting, and when available, surrender. When there are more 10s than normal, intelligent use of these options become even more valuable to the player with the added bonus that the player gets paid 3 to 2 on his blackjacks while the dealer only gets even-money.

The dealer, on the other hand, must play by the prescribed rules of the game and has none of these options. He must draw to hands 16 or below and stand on 17 or higher.

Our count strategy shows us when there are more 10 value cards in the deck than normal and then shows us how to take advantage of this situation. Let's move on now and learn how to count cards.

THE BASIC COUNT STRATEGY (LEVEL I)

Following are the values each card will be given upon its removal from the deck of cards.

2	3	4	5	6	7	8	9	10	A
0	+1	+1	+1	+1	0	0	0	-1	0

Notice that the count is balanced: four cards are assigned +1 values, the 3s, 4s, 5s and 6s, and four cards are assigned -1 values, the 10s, Js, Qs and Ks. (The 2s and 7s are less valuable for the player when removed, and are thus excluded from the count.)

Looking at the values assigned, you can see that 10s are valuable cards for the player to have in the deck, their removal assigned a "-" value, and the small cards, 3, 4, 5 and 6, are favorable to the player when removed, their removal assigned a "+" value.

Thus, when the count is plus, the player has the advantage, and when the count is minus, the house has the edge. Simple enough. The 0 value cards have a smaller effect on your chances of winning and are given these neutral values.

The one exception is the Ace. While misleadingly assigned a 0 value in the count, the Ace is actually a valuable card for the player.

Understanding the Ace in the Count

Since the Ace sometimes has the properties of a high card and other times, the properties of a small card (eleven points or one point), we receive misleading information from our count should the Ace be included, and thus we keep track of it on the side.

For example, the hand 12 vs. the dealer's 4. For playing strategy purposes, the Ace acts as a small card in this and other similar situations. However, if we included the Ace in the count, the count would see the Ace as a high card and advanced players would have a much less accurate read on proper play.

(With a side count of Aces, advanced players also enjoy more accuracy on insurance decisions.)

However, since the Ace is important for betting purposes, giving us a valuable 3 to 2 payoff when a blackjack is dealt, a bonus the dealer doesn't enjoy, we will keep a side count of Aces (later on), and bring our betting efficiency up to 96%. We will show you how to use the Ace for betting when we discuss the *Level II Count*.

The Running Count

Off the top of the deck, our count always begins at 0. As cards are removed from play, we'll add or subtract the values assigned to cards such that you keep *only one number* in your head at any time.

Here's how the count works. We'll adjust our count each time cards are removed from play. Thus, if a 3 is removed, our count becomes +1. If a 6 is then removed from play, the count becomes +2 (+1 and +1). A Jack is then played, making the count +1 (+2 and -1).

We call this count the **running count**.

If two 10s are now removed, the running count, or count, becomes -1 (+1 and -2). The removal of an Ace and a 7 keep the count at -1 since both cards are assigned neutral values.

The count tells us our relative advantage to the house before the cards are dealt and we'll take advantage of it by making bigger bets when we have the edge and smaller bets when the house enjoys the edge.

Fluctuations In the Count

In a single deck game, you can expect fluctuations between + or -6 or greater. In multiple deck games, the fluctuation will be greater, sometimes as high as + or - 20.

Practicing the Count

Before using the count in a casino, you should feel comfortable using it at home. First of all, you'll need a deck of cards.

After learning the number values of the Basic Count Strategy, go through a deck of cards one card at a time, and practice keeping the count. If your count is +1 when you reach the last card, then that card should be a ten value card, if -1, a small card (3, 4, 5 or 6), and if 0, that last card should be a neutral value card (2, 7, 8, 9 or Ace). If something is off, either the deck is short or you have made a mistake.

Do this three times perfectly. After you have done so, repeat the above procedure turning over two cards at a time.

When you are comfortable with these steps, you are ready to try your skills under actual casino conditions.

The True Count

While our running count tells us the relationship between ten value cards and small cards, our indicator of favorability, it does not give us an accurate picture of that relationship to the total amount of cards in the deck or decks. For example, removing two cards from a pack of 208 cards (four decks) is not as significant as removing two cards from only 52, which in turn is not as weighty as that removal from only 20 cards. The smaller the pack of cards, the more sensitive the deck or decks are to particular card removal.

The **true count** makes this adjustment for us, and tells us how favorable the running count actually is.

The Basic Count Strategy is based on the half deck level. For every deck of cards we have two half decks. Thus, a two deck game contains four half decks, a four deck game contains eight half decks, a six deck game, 12 half decks, and so on. We work with a half deck level as opposed to a full deck level in order to maintain more accuracy in our count.

To figure the true count, we divide the running count by the number of half decks remaining. For example, if the running count is +6 and six half decks remain to be played, than we divide +6 by six (half decks) to get a true count of +1. If that same +6 is achieved when 3 half decks remain to be played, the true count is then +2. If just one half deck remains, dividing by one, we get a true count of +6.

It doesn't matter how many decks the game started with: The true count only measures the cards remaining to be played.

What do we do if the numbers don't divide easily? No problem - we approximate. If the running count is +7 and three half decks remain to be played, our true count would be +2 for betting purposes. An exact true count figure is not necessary.

Keep Only One Number In Your Head

It is important to keep only one number in your head, the *running count* number. We use the true count to determine just how favorable our situation is and bet accordingly. We also use it to figure out the ratio of 10s to non-tens so our strategy can be adjusted.

Once your true count adjustment has been made for the proper betting or strategy decision, forget the true count number.

Thought processes:

1. Are we in a favorable situation?

If yes, meaning the running count is +, we know that we probably want to bet more than our minimum. (In a multiple deck game we want to wait until the *true count* reaches +1 before raising our bet).

If no, meaning the count is neutral or -, then we want to make our minimum bet.

2. How favorable is the situation?

Is the true count stronger or weaker than the running count indicates? If we are at the half deck level, we know the true count is exactly equal to the running count.

If more than a half deck remains (which will be almost always the case in a four, six or eight deck game), than the true count will not be as strong as the running count, and we'll have to divide our running count number by the approximate half decks remaining. We intuitively know that a +4 running count is less than a +4 true count with more than a half deck remaining to be played.

Conversely, if the level of cards has dipped below the half deck mark, which is a usual occurrence in a single deck game, the true count number will be stronger than the running count, and if the deck is positive, we'll certainly be aggressive in our betting.

The fewer the number of cards that remain, that is, the deeper into the deck the game goes, the more powerful the running count.

True Count Betting - Single Deck Game

In a single deck game, the opening or neutral wager can be one or two units. Theoretically, since the game is about even at this point, three or four units can be wagered, but for money management purposes, you want to keep your bets smaller at this point and wait for the count to become positive before raising bets.

Once the count shifts in the player's favor, you have the advantage and want to bet at least two units. As the advantage increases in blackjack, so does our bet, as will be seen.

The Single Deck Bet Range chart following shows the optimal betting range for a single deck blackjack game and is based on the *True Count*.

Single Deck Bet Range	
True Count	**Bet**
-*	1 unit
0	1 or 2 units
+1	2 units
+2	3 units
+3	4 units
+4	5 units
+5 or more	5 units
*On any minus count (-), bet the minimum amount, 1 unit.	

True Count Betting - Multiple Deck Game

In a multiple deck game we need a more aggressive betting ratio to overcome the initial advantage the house has over the player. The player should keep to his minimum one unit bet until the **true count** is +1 or greater. It sometimes takes a while in the multiple deck game before the count is sufficiently positive to overcome the disadvantage of playing with the larger number of cards. However, once the true count reaches +1, we begin to have the edge over the casino and should start increasing our bets.

The player should try to get a bet ratio of 1-6 or 1-7 units in a double deck game, and if possible, at least 1-10 units in a four deck game, and 1-14 is a six deck game.

Since the house enjoy a slight initial edge in multiple deck games, playing Las Vegas Strip rules, we want to make our opening bet as small as possible - a minimum one unit bet. Once the true count gets favorable, we'll increase our bets.

The Multiple Deck Bet Range chart following shows the optimal betting range for a multiple deck blackjack game and like the single deck chart, is based on the *True Count*.

Multiple Deck Bet Range	
True Count	Bet
-*	1 unit
0	1 unit
+1	2 units
+2	3 units
+3	5 units
+4	7 units
+5	9 units
+6	11 units
+7	13 units
+8	15 units
+9	17 units
+10	20 units
*On any minus count (-), bet the minimum amount, 1 unit.	

Practical Betting and Profit Expectation

The bet sizes for the particular true count numbers in the single and multiple deck bet range charts are formulated to give the player the optimal profit expectation results while limiting his risk factor. As you can see, the greater our advantage, the more we will bet. But there's more involved in casino blackjack.

It is not always possible to bet ideally in blackjack, for the casino will bar players they feel can beat them, and often, part of a smart player's game is in disguising that fact. Neither memorization of the numbers above or betting exactly according to the units shown is important - you need only approximate these numbers to enjoy a healthy edge.

The primary factor affecting your profit expectation at blackjack is your bet range, the difference between what you bet when the house has the edge and how much you bet when the advantage swings in favor of the player.

Thus, if you bet more when you have the edge and less when the house enjoys that advantage, play the basic strategies perfectly and exercise sound money management, you'll have an advantage over the casino, and in the long run, you'll be a winner at blackjack.

Insurance

In Basic Strategy we learned that Insurance was a bad wager. However, now that we are equipped with a strategy that provides information on ten density, we will sometimes find the Insurance bet to be a profitable wager for the player.

In a single deck game, take Insurance whenever the ***True Count*** is greater than or equal to +1. In a multiple deck game, take Insurance whenever the ***True Count*** is greater than or equal to +1 1/2.

LEVEL II COUNT STRATEGY

Before you learn how to adjust your betting for Ace richness or poorness, make sure you're completely comfortable with all the other strategies; the Optimal Basic Strategies and the Level I strategies - the Basic Count Strategy, the Running Count and the True Count Adjustment.

Though it is not absolutely necessary that the bettor keep a side count of Aces, we recommend that it be done after being completely proficient with the other strategies, for it will give you an extra edge over the casino.

The A-B-C-D Adjustment

We recommend that the player use the alphabet for the Ace Count. In a single deck game, count A, B, C and D for each Ace removed, and in a multiple deck game, extend the letters, so that the 16th Ace removed in a four deck game is given a P value.

This way you don't confuse the letters with the numbers. With a +3 count and five Aces removed, the player would have the count as 3E. You may also use numbers as you do with the count, positions of your feet or chips, or numerous other creative ideas you may come up with - whatever works is fine.

There are four Aces in a single deck, eight in a double deck, sixteen in four decks and twenty four in six decks, an average of one Ace per thirteen cards. As cards come into play the normal composition of Aces change. When the deck contains a higher density of Aces than one per thirteen, the normal composition of a full deck, the deck is said to be **Ace-rich**, a favorable situation for the player. Conversely, a lower density of Aces, called an **Ace-poor** deck, is unfavorable for the player.

To accommodate the Ace factor into our count, we add +1 to the running count for every Ace that the deck is rich, and subtract 1 for every Ace that the deck is poor. Note that this is only a mental adjustment to be made before the true count adjustment, and subsequent bet is placed.

Let's look at an example to make this perfectly clear. The running count is +4D in a four deck game and two decks remain to be played. Since only four Aces (D) have been used in two decks instead of the eight expected, the deck is Ace-rich by four Aces. Making a *quick mental adjustment*, we add the 4 extra Aces and get an adjusted running count of +8.

Four half decks remain giving us a true count of +2 for betting purposes (+8 divided by four 1/2 decks). We make the bet according to the +4 adjusted count. We'll immediately return to the original running count figure of +4D, the only number we retain.

Simplified Winning Approach

If making the true count and side ace count adjustments prove too taxing for your style of play, you can still enjoy an edge with a simplified approach.

Basically, the key to beating the house at blackjack is to bet more when you have the edge and less when the house has an edge. The running count gives us this information, and thus becomes the most important count for us to concentrate on.

Plus (+) means we have the edge. Minus (-) means the house has the edge. With a minus running count, you'll always make the minimum bet, while with a plus count, you'll gauge the true count level, and size your increased bet accordingly.

Winning Summary

We've covered a lot of ground in this section, showing you how to play your hands, how to optimally use all the options available at blackjack, plus given you the beginning steps toward being a successful card counter with Levels I and II of a card counting strategy.

A lot of money can be made at blackjack, which is why the game is so popular, but as you see, you must invest a little time in learning how to play the game properly.

If this section has whetted your appetite toward making money at blackjack, following are two options for players: the first a winning method for players who want to win without counting, the second, much more powerful, the very strategy that I use to win money at blackjack.

Winning Without Counting Cards

For those who find that counting cards is not their cup of tea, we've developed a simple-to-use but effective non-counting strategy, the Cardoza 1,2,3 Multiple Deck Non-Counter. This brand new strategy, developed for the first time in 1992, shows you how to beat the single or multiple deck game without the mental effort necessary for a count strategy and actually gives you an edge of about 1/2 - 1%.

Non-counting blackjack players need no longer be intimidated, for they can now enjoy the mathematical edge over the casino in multiple deck games.

The ad in the back of the book gives you more information on one of the most important breakthroughs in blackjack in the last 10 years.

MAKING EVEN MORE MONEY AT BLACKJACK

In this section we've shown you Levels I and II of the count strategy, enough to get you going with a basic edge over the casino. However, if you're a serious player and want to really get the edge over the casino and be a consistent winner at blackjack, you'll want to immediately get to work and learn the full counting strategy.

Counting cards is easy, and with a little practice anyone can do it. However, you must learn the proper order of counting cards so that the count is kept accurately, and equally important, you must know insider techniques such as *card cancelling*, which make card counting simple under actual casino conditions.

The **Cardoza Base Count Strategy** package and the **Master Lesson Plans** advertised in the back reveal all these important concepts and show you how to have the maximum edge possible at blackjack. You'll learn advanced betting and playing strategies, plus how to adjust your hand depending upon the count. Full strategy charts prepare you for every situation. No longer will those 15s and 16s be busted with big bets on the table!

I've made my living playing blackjack in the casinos. In fact, no casino will knowingly deal cards to me, and many of them have banned me from playing blackjack at their tables. You can be a good player as well. These strategies will show you the exact system I use.

See ads for the Cardoza Base Count Strategy and Master Lesson Plans in the back of the book for details. (Also look for the special bonuses to readers of this book.)

Money can be made at blackjack, and as I tell all my students
- Good Skill!

PLAYING CRAPS TO WIN

INTRODUCTION

Craps is the most exciting of the casino games, for the action is fast, and a player catching a good roll can win large sums of money quickly. But big money can be lost just as fast unless the player is conversant with the best bets available and knows how to use them in a coordinated strategy.

We'll go over the fundamentals of playing casino craps in this section, and not only explain all the bets available and show you which wagers are the best to make, but also, we'll show you how to play these bets so that when the smoke clears, you'll have the best chances of emerging a winner.

Let's get on with it, and let the dice roll!

BEGINNER'S GUIDE TO CASINO CRAPS

The Table

The standard casino craps table is rectangular in shape and depending upon the particular size of the casino's table, is built to accommodate between 15 to 24 players. The sides of the table are several feet above the layout where the bets are made, giving the players an edge to lean on, and giving the dice walls to carom off.

The Layout

The craps layout is divided into three distinct sections. The two end sections, which are identical, are areas around which the players cluster, and where the majority of bets are made. Each end area is run by one of the standing dealers.

The middle area is flanked on either side by a boxman and stickman. This area contains the proposition, or center bets, and is completely under the jurisdiction of the stickman.

The layout is a large piece of green felt with various imprints marking the plethora of bets possible. All action is centered on the layout. Bets are placed, paid off and collected on this felt surface. And, of course, it is on the layout where the dice are thrown.

Layouts around the world are basically the same. Though some clubs may have slight variations, none of these need concern us, for the game of craps is basically the same whatever casino you play in. The minor variations that do occur, concern bets whose odds are so poor that we wouldn't want to make them anyway.

Nevada Craps Layout

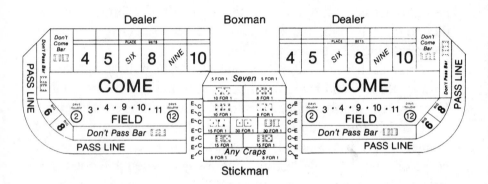

The Dice

The game of craps is played with two six-sided dice, with each die numbered from 1 to 6. The dice are manufactured so that they fall as randomly as possible, with a 5 being just as likely to fall on one die as a 3. However, we'll see later that combining two dice together creates some combinations that are more likely to appear than others, and this is the basis of the odds in craps.

Players

Only one player is needed to play craps, while as many as can fit around a craps table are the maximum. When the action is hot and heavy, bettors will be lined up shoulder to shoulder, screaming, yelling and cajoling, for the dice to come through and make them winners.

Casino Personnel

The average craps table is manned by a crew of four casino employees - one stickman, who stands at the center of the table, two dealers, who stand on the opposite side of the stickman at either end of the table, and a boxman who is seated between the two standing dealers and directly across from the stickman.

Let's look at the function of each crewman in turn.

The Stickman

The **stickman's** main responsibility is the handling of the dice, a task he performs with a flexible, hooked stick. When a new shooter is coming-out, the stickman will offer him a cache of dice to choose from, and after two have been selected, will return the remaining dice to his box.

After each roll of the dice, the stickman will announce the number thrown and bring the dice back to the center of the table. Usually, he'll supply additional information about its consequences.

If a 7 is thrown on the come-out roll, he may announce, "7, winner on the pass line." If instead, a 2, 3 or 12 is rolled on the come-out, he may say, "Craps, line away." When a shooter sevens-out, the stickman might exclaim, "7 out, line away."

A good stickman is a show in himself. He generates excitement and makes the game more lively and colorful for both the players and the dealers. And from the casino's standpoint, happy players tend to bet heavier and wilder than they normally would.

The dice will be returned to the shooter after the dealers have finished making payoffs.

The stickman is also responsible for the proposition, or center bets made in the middle of the layout. He will place all proposition bets directed his way into their proper location on the layout.

If these bets are winners, the stickman will direct the dealers to pay off the winning players, and if the bets are losers, he will collect the lost bets and push them over to the boxman.

The Dealers

There is a dealer located on either side of the boxman, and his main responsibility is to handle all the monetary transactions and betting on his end of the table. He pays off winning bets and collects losing ones, converts cash into chips, and will change chips into higher or lower denominations for the player.

Though the player can make many of the bets himself, there are wagers such as the place bets and certain free-odds bets which must be given to the dealer to be placed.

Each standing dealer has a **marker buck**, a plastic disk used to indicate the established point. If a player is coming-out, beginning his roll, the marker buck will be lying on its black side, labeled "**off**," and if a point is established, the dealer will flip the marker buck to the white side, marked "**on**," and place it in the appropriately numbered box to indicate the point. It is with the dealers that the player will have most of his contact and to whom he can address his questions.

The Boxman

The **boxman** sits between the two dealers and across from the stickman, and from this central position, supervises the running of the craps table. His job is not only to watch over the casinos bankroll, most of which sits right in front of him in huge stacks, but to make sure the dealers make the correct payoffs so that neither the player nor the house gets shorted.

In addition to the boxmen, there are other supervisors, called floormen and pit bosses, who watch over the action from behind the boxman in the area known as the pit.

Entering a Game

To enter a craps game, slip into a space by the rail of the craps table. After catching the dealer's attention, place your cash on the layout and inform him of the denomination of chips you would like. The dealer will take your money, and give it to the boxman who will supervise the exchange.

Tipping

Tips are shared by the crew working the craps table. Though

the usual tip is to make a proposition bet, with the exclamation "one for the boys," a better way to toke the crew would be to make a line bet for them, so they can have a good chance of winning the bet.

Dealers prefer this type of tip for they too are aware how poor the proposition bets are. This is also better than just handing over the toke, for if the bet is won, the dealer wins double for the tip - the amount bet for him plus the winnings from that bet.

Play of the Game and the Come-Out Roll

When a new player is to throw the dice, the stickman will empty his box of dice and push them across the layout with his stick. After this player, known as the **shooter**, selects two dice of his choice, the stickman will retrieve the remaining dice and return them to his box.

In a new game, the player closest to the boxman's left side will receive the dice first, and the rotation of the dice will go clockwise from player to player around the craps table.

The shooter has no advantage over the other players except perhaps the psychological edge he may get throwing the dice himself. He is required to make either a pass or don't pass bet as the shooter, and in addition, can make any other bets allowed.

There are a wide variety of bets the players can make, and these bets should be placed before the shooter throws the dice. Players can bet with the dice or against them at their preference, but in either case, the casino will book all wagers.

Play is ready to begin.

The shooter is supposed to throw the dice so that they bounce off the far wall of the table. If the throw does not reach the far wall, the shooter will be requested to toss harder on his next throw, and if he persist in underthrowing the dice, the boxman may disallow him from throwing further.

This policy protects against cheats that can manipulate unobstructed throws of the dice.

The first throw is called the **come-out roll**, and is the most significant roll in craps. It marks the first roll of a shoot, and can either become an automatic winner or loser for players betting with the dice, called **right bettors**, or those betting against the dice, called **wrong bettors**, or establish a point with which the shooter hopes to repeat before a 7 is thrown.

The come-out roll works as follows. The throw of a 7 or 11 on the come-out roll is an automatic winner for the pass line bettors, players betting that the dice will win, or pass, while the throw of a **craps**, a 2, 3 or 12 is an automatic loser.

For the don't pass bettors, those betting against the dice, the come-out roll works almost exactly opposite to the pass line bet. A come-out roll of a 7 or an 11 is an automatic loser, a 2 or a 3 an automatic winner, while the 12 (in some casinos a 2 instead) is a standoff.

If the come-out roll is an automatic decision, a 2, 3, 7, 11 or 12, the affected players will have their bets paid or collected, and the following roll will be a new come-out roll.

Any other number thrown, a 4, 5, 6, 8, 9 or 10, becomes the **point**, and the dealers will indicate this by flipping their respective marker bucks to the white side marked "on," and move the disk into the rectangular numbered boxes corresponding to the point number thrown.

The shoot will continue until either the point is repeated, a winner for the pass line bettors and a loser for the don't pass bettors, or until a seven is thrown, known as **sevening-out**, a loser on the pass line and winner on the don't pass. In either case, the shoot will have been completed, and the following roll will be a new come-out roll, the start of a new shoot.

Once a point is established, only the 7 and the point are consequential rolls for the pass and don't pass bettors, also called **line bettors**. All other rolls are neutral throws for these bets.

There are many other bets available to the player as we will discuss later, some that can be made only after a point is established, and others that can be made at any time during a shoot. So while the line bettors may not be affected by a particular throw, the dealers may be paying off or collecting chips on other affected wagers while the shoot is in progress.

The shooter can continue throwing the dice until he sevens-out. Then, after all affected bets are settled on the layout, the stickman will present his collection of dice to the next player in a clockwise rotation. Even though the shooter may **crap-out** (the throw of a 2, 3 or 12) on his come-out roll, a losing roll for the pass line bettors, the shooter does not have to yield the dice. It is only when he throws a 7 before his point repeats, *sevens-out*, that the dice must be relinquished.

The Come-Out Roll Capsulated

The come-out roll occurs when:

1 - A new shooter takes the dice.

2 - The shooter throws a 2, 3, 7, 11 or 12 on the come-out roll, an automatic winner or loser for the line bettors.

3 - After a point is established, the shooter either repeats that point or sevens-out.

Betting Right or Wrong

Betting right or wrong are only casino terms used to designate whether a player is betting with the dice, **betting right**, or betting against the dice, **betting wrong**, and are in no way indicative of a correct or incorrect way of playing. As we shall see, both ways of betting are equally valid.

UNDERSTANDING THE ODDS

Craps is played with two dice, individually called die, and each die is a near perfect six sided cube, guaranteed to be within 1/10,000 of an inch accurate.

Each die has six equally possible outcomes when thrown - numbers one through six. The two dice thrown together have a total of 36 possible outcomes, the six combinations of one die by the six combinations of the other. The chart on the following page shows these combinations.

Dice Combinations Chart	
Result	**Odds of Result**
2	1 out of 36
3	2 out of 36
4	3 out of 36
5	4 out of 36
6	5 out of 36
7	6 out of 36
8	5 out of 36
9	4 out of 36
10	3 out of 36
11	2 out of 36
12	1 out of 36
Total	**36 out of 36**

You can see by the chart that the 7 is more likely to be thrown than any other number, having six possible combinations. Next in frequency are the 6 and 8, five outcomes each, the 5 and 9, four outcomes, the 4 and 10, three outcomes apiece, the 3 and 11, two outcomes, and finally, the 2 and the 12, one combination each.

A Shortcut to Remembering the Odds

Notice the symmetry of combinations on either side of the 7. The 6 and 8 have equal possibilities of being thrown, just as the 5 and 9, 4 and 10, 3 and 11, and 2 and 12 do.

If you take rolls of 7 and below and subtract one from that number, you arrive at the correct number of combinations for that roll. Thus, there are four ways to roll a 5 (5-1), six ways to roll a 7 (7-1) and one way to roll a 2 (2-1).

For numbers greater than the 7, match that number with the corresponding symmetrical number on the other side of the 7, and subtract one. Thus, to find the combinations of the 8, you match it with the 6 (which has an equal likelihood of occurring), and subtracting one, you get five combinations.

Figuring the Odds of Rolling a Specific Number

To figure the odds of rolling any particular number, divide the number of combinations for that particular number into 36, the total number of combinations possible.

Let's say the 7. There are six ways to roll a 7. Dividing the six combinations into 36, the total number of combinations, we find the odds of rolling a 7 on any one roll is one in six (6/36 reduced to 1/6), or equivalently, 5 to 1. The chart below shows the odds of rolling a number on any one roll.

Odds of Rolling the Numbers			
	Combinations	Chance of Being Rolled	Expressed in Odds
2 or 12	1	1/36	35 to 1
3 or 11	2	2/36	17 to 1
4 or 10	3	3/36	11 to 1
5 or 9	4	4/36	8 to 1
6 or 8	5	5/36	6 .2 to 1
7	6	6/36	5 to 1

Understanding The Terminology -
Correct Odds, House Payoff and Edge

The house advantage or edge is the difference between the player's chances of winning the bet, called the **correct odds**, and the casino's actual payoff, called the **house payoff** or simply, the **payoff**. For example, the correct odds of rolling a 7 are 5 to 1. Since the house will pay only 4 to 1 should the 7 be thrown, they maintain an edge of 16.67 percent on this wager.

To play craps intelligently and better understand the choices available to him, the player must first and foremost be aware of the house advantage on every bet he will ever make, for that, in the long run, determines the player's chances of winning.

Five for One, Five to One

Sometimes on a layout you will see payoffs represented as *for* instead of the usual *to*, such as 9 for 1. This means that the payoff will be a total of nine units, eight winning chips along with your original bet, a house subterfuge to increase its edge over the player. The usual 9 to 1 payoff means nine winning chips and your original bet returned, for a total of 10 units.

Beware of any payoffs with the *for*. As a rule, this type of bet has poor odds to begin with and we wouldn't want to make it anyway, with the to or the for.

The Bets

Craps offers the player a wide variety of possible wagers, with each bet having its own characteristics and inherent odds. Some bets, which we will refer to as **sequence bets**, may require a series of rolls before the outcome is determined, while the outcome of others, called **one-roll bets**, is determined on the very next roll.

Some bets are paid off by the house at **even-money**; for every dollar wagered, the player wins a dollar, while other bets have payoffs as high as 30 to 1. However, as you will see, generally the higher the house payoff, the worse the odds are.

And the odds of the bet, that is, the mathematical house return on every dollar wagered, is the most important concern of the player. To have the best chances of winning, you must avoid all the sucker bets, and make only the best bets available.

THE BEST BETS

The bets in this section have the lowest built-in house edge of all the bets in craps, and one bet, the free-odds, gives the house no advantage whatsoever. These wagers, the pass, don't pass, come, don't come and the free-odds bets, are the most important bets a player can make, and are the foundation of our winning strategies.

The Line Bets - Pass and Don't Pass

These even-money bets can only be made on a come-out roll, before a point is established, and give the house an edge of only 1.4 percent. And when backed by the free-odds wagers, the overall house edge drops to 0.8 percent in a single odds game and to 0.6 percent in a double odds game.

Pass Line

Players making pass line bets are wagering that the dice will **pass**, or win, and are called right bettors. Pass line bets are also referred to as **front line bets**, and are made by placing the wager in the area marked pass line.

On the come-out roll, a throw of a 7 or 11 is an automatic winner for the pass line bettors while the throw of a craps, a 2, 3 or 12 is an automatic loser. If any other number is thrown, the 4, 5, 6, 8, 9 or 10, then that number is established as the point, and the shooter must repeat the point before a 7 is thrown for pass line bettors to win. The throw of a 7 before the point repeats is a loser for pass line bettors, called **sevening-out**, and the dealers will collect the lost bets.

Once the point is established, only the 7 and the point number affect the pass line bettor. All other numbers have no bearing on the bet and can be considered neutral throws.

Pass Line Capsulated

Payoff: Even -Money   **House Edge**: 1.4%

Automatic Winners - 7 or 11 on the come-out roll.

Automatic Losers - 2,3, or 12 on the come-out roll.

Once a point is established on the come-out roll,
the pass line bettor:

Wins by the point repeating before the 7 is thrown.

Loses by the roll of a 7 before the point repeats.

Let's look at three progressions to see how the pass line bet works.

1. The come-out roll is a 5, establishing 5 as the point. The following roll is a 2, a neutral throw, for a point has already been established. An 8 is then thrown, also neutral, and then a 5. The point was repeated, or made, before the seven was thrown, and the pass line bettors win their bets.

2. The come-out roll is a 7, an automatic winner for the pass line bettors. Since the progression is completed, the following roll will be another come-out roll.

3. Here's a losing proposition. The come-out roll is a 9, establishing 9 as the point. The shooter then rolls a 6, 12, and 11, all neutral rolls since a point is already established. Then a 7 is thrown. Since the 7 was rolled before the 9, the shooter's point repeated, pass line bettors lose and the dealer will collect their bets. A new come-out roll will ensue.

Don't Pass

Players betting don't pass are called wrong bettors, and are betting against the dice. Don't pass bets are also called **back line bets** and are made by placing the wager in the area marked *don't pass*.

On the come-out roll, a throw of a 2 or 3 is an automatic winner for the don't pass bettors, while a 7 or an 11 is an automatic loser. The 12 is a standoff between the back line bettor and the house. (In some casinos the 2 is the standoff and the 12 is the automatic winner. Either way it makes no difference, for there is only one way to throw the 2 or 12.)

Once the point is established, don't pass bettors win by having the 7 thrown before the shooter repeats his point, and lose by the point being repeated before the shooter sevens-out.

Don't Pass Line Capsulated
Payoff: Even-Money   **House Edge**: 1.4%
Automatic Winners - 2 (or 12) and 3 on the come-out roll.
Automatic Losers - 7 or 11 on the come-out roll.
Standoff - 12 (or 2 in some casinos) on the come-out roll.
Once a point is established on the come-out roll
don't pass bettors:
Wins by the throw of a 7 before the point repeats.
Loses by the point repeating before the 7 thrown.

Here are some progressions to illustrate the don't pass wager.

1. The come-out roll is a 6, establishing 6 as the point. The following rolls are a 5 (no bearing on the outcome), then a 12 (still no bearing) and then a 7. Since the 7 was rolled before the 6 repeated, don't pass bettors win.

2. The come-out roll is a 3, an automatic winner for the don't pass bettor.

3. The come-out roll is a 4, establishing 4 as the point. A 3 is then rolled (neutral), and then a 4, a loss for the back line bettors since the point repeated before the 7 was rolled.

Come and Don't Come Bets

The come and don't come bets work according to the same rules as the pass and don't pass bets except that the come and don't come bets can only be made *after* a point is established. The line bets, on the other hand, can only be placed on a come-out roll, before a point is established.

The advantage of these bets are that they allow the player to cover more points as a right or wrong bettor at the same low 1.4% house edge. And like the line bets, the overall house edge drops to 0.8% when backed by single odds, and 0.6% when backed by double odds.

Come bets are made by putting the chips into the area marked *come*, while don't come bets are placed in the *don't come box*. Won bets are paid at even-money.

Come Bets

We follow the play of the come bets just as we would with the pass line bets. A 7 or 11 on the first throw following the placing of the bet is an automatic winner, while a 2, 3 or 12 in an automatic loser. Any other number thrown, the 4, 5, 6, 8, 9 or 10, becomes the point for that come bet, called the **come point**, and the dealer will move the bet from the come box into the large rectangular numbered boxes located at the top of the layout to mark the come point.

Once the come point is established, the bet is won if the come point repeats before the shooter sevens-out, and lost if the 7 is rolled before the point repeats. All other throws are inconsequential on this bet. Won bets will be paid off and removed from the layout.

The bettor can make continuous come bets until all the points are covered if he desires. Thus, it is possible for the throw of a 7 to simultaneously wipe out several established come bets. On the other hand, a hot shooter rolling point numbers can bring frequent winners to the aggressive come bettor.

Let's follow a progression where the right bettor makes both pass line and come bets.

Player Bets $5 on the pass line. *The come-out roll is a 5*, establishing 5 as the point.

Player Bets $5 on the come. *The roll is an 8*, establishing 8 as the come point. The dealer moves the $5 come bet to the rectangular box marked 8 to indicate that 8 is the point for that come bet. In effect, the player has two points working, the 5 and the 8, and decides to make another come bet.

Player Bets $5 on the come. *The roll is a 6*. The dealer moves this new bet to the 6, the come point for this bet. The other two points are not affected by this roll. The player has three points established, the 5, 6 and 8, and makes no more bets at this time.

The roll is a 5, a $5 winner on the pass line. It is paid off and removed from the layout, leaving the player with two come points, the 6 and 8.

Player Bets $5 on the pass line. Since the next roll is a come-out roll and the player wants to cover another point, he bets the pass. *The roll is a 10*, establishing 10 as the point.

Player makes no additional bets at this time. *The roll is a 2* (neutral on all established bets), then *an 8 is thrown*, a $5 winner on the come point of 8, and that bet is paid off and removed.

The following roll is not a come-out roll, for the come point was made, not the pass line point, the 10.

Player Bets $5 on the come. *The roll is a 7*. While the 7 is a $5 winner for the new come bet, it is a loser for the two established points, and they are removed from the layout by the dealer.

The roll of the 7 cleared the layout, and the following roll will be a new come-out roll.

Don't Come Bets

Like the don't pass wager, a 7 or 11 on the first roll following a don't come bet is an automatic loser and the 2 and 3 are automatic winners, 12 being a standoff. (In casinos where the 2 is a standoff and the 12 a winner on the don't pass, the same will hold true for the don't come bets.)

If a 4, 5, 6, 8, 9 or 10 is thrown, establishing a point for the don't come bet, the dealer will move the chips behind the appropriate point box to mark the don't come point. Don't come bettors now win by having the 7 thrown before that point is made. Other numbers, as with the don't pass bets, are neutral rolls. Only the 7 and the come point determine the bet.

Let's follow a progression where the wrong bettor makes both don't pass and don't come bets.

Player Bets $5 on the don't pass. *The roll is a 10*, establishing 10 as the point.

Player Bets $5 on the don't come, continuing to bet against the dice. *The roll is a 2*, a $5 winner on the new don't come bet, and that bet is paid off and removed.

Player Bets $5 on the don't come. *The roll is a 6*. The dealer moves the bet from the don't come area to the upper section of the box numbered 6 to indicate that 6 is the point for this don't come bet. The player now has two points working, the 10 and 6, and decides to establish a third point.

Player Bets $5 on the don't come. *The roll is a 10*, a $5 loser on the don't pass since the point repeated before a 7 was thrown. The don't come point of 6 is unaffected, and the new don't come bet is moved to the 10 box, since 10 is the come point for the new don't come wager.

The player decides not to make any more bets, but if he did, he would bet don't pass for the next throw is a come-out roll. *The roll is 7*, winner on both come points, and they are paid off and removed. The next roll will be a new come-out roll.

Free-Odds Bets

Though not indicated anywhere on the layout, the **free-odds** or **odds** bets are the best bets a player can make at craps, and are an indispensable part of any winning strategy. The free-odds bets are so named, for, unlike the other bets at craps, the house has no advantage over the player. Hence, the term free-odds.

However, to make a free-odds bet, the player must first have placed a pass, don't pass, come or don't come wager, and in a sense, is backing those bets, for the free-odds bet can only be made in conjunction with these wagers.

When backed by single odds, the overall odds of the pass, don't pass, come and don't come bets drop to 0.8%, and where double odds are allowed and utilized, the overall odds drop to only 0.6% against the player.

These are the best odds a player can get at craps.

Free-Odds · Pass Line

Once a point is established on the come-out roll, the pass line bettor can make a **free-odds bet**, and is betting that his point will repeat before a 7 is thrown.

This bet is paid off at the correct odds, giving the house no edge, and is made by placing the chips behind the pass line wager and just outside the pass line area.

Pass Line and Free-Odds Bet

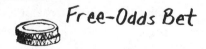

When single odds are allowed, the player can bet up to the amount wagered on his pass line bet, and in certain instances he can bet more. And when double odds are allowed, the player can bet twice his pass line bet as a free-odds wager.

Though the player can bet less than the permissible amount on the free-odds wager and is allowed to reduce or remove this bet at any time, he should never do so, for the free-odds bets are the most advantageous bets in craps, and should be fully taken advantage of.

Following is a table which shows the correct odds of the point repeating before a 7 is thrown and the house payoff. Note how the house takes no percentage advantage on these bets since the pay-off is identical to the correct odds.

Odds of Point Repeating Before a Seven		
Point Number	Correct Odds	House Payoff
4 or 10	2 to 1	2 to 1
5 or 9	3 to 2	3 to 2
6 or 8	6 to 5	6 to 5

The odds presented in this table are easy to figure for the only numbers that affect the free-odds bet are the point number, which is a winner, and the 7, which is a loser. All other throws are inconsequential.

There are three ways to roll a winning 4 or 10, and six ways to roll a losing 7, thus 2 to 1 is the correct odds on points 4 or 10. A 5 or 9 can be rolled four ways each against the same six ways of rolling a 7, thus the correct odds are 3 to 2 against the 5 or 9. A 6 or 8 can be made by five combinations, and again, since there are six ways to roll a losing 7, the correct odds are 6 to 5 against the 6 or 8.

Special Allowances - Single Odds Game

To make the payoffs easier, most casinos allow the player to make a single odds bet greater than his pass line (or come) bet in the following instances.

a. With a pass line bet such as $5 or $25 and the point being a 5 or 9, the casino will allow the player to make an odds bet of $6 and $30 respectively behind the line. If the bet is won, the 3 to 2 payoff on the $6 free-odds bet would be $9, and on the $30 bet, $45.

Without this special allowance, the player would be unable to get the full correct odds on the $5 or $25 free-odds bet since the $1 or more minimum craps tables do not deal in half dollars.

b. With a three unit bet such as $3 or $15, and the point being a 6 or 8, the casino allows a five unit free-odds bet behind the line thus permitting the player to take full advantage of the 6 to 5 payoff on points 6 and 8. In the above examples, $5 and $25 free-odds bets would be permitted, and if won, would pay the player $6 and $30 respectively.

A three unit bet translates to $3 for the $1 bettor, $15 for the $5 bettor, $30 for the $10 bettor, and so on. Any bet that can be divisible by three can be considered a three unit bet and be backed by the special allowance single odds bets.

A $30 bet on the pass line can be backed by only $30 if the point is a 5 or 9 since the 3 to 2 payoff can be made on this amount, but if the point is a 6 or an 8, can be backed by $50 (five unit special allowance). If uncertain about the amounts you are allowed to bet, check with the dealer.

No special allowances are allowed when the 4 or 10 are points for they are easily paid off at 2 to 1 no matter the bet.

On bets smaller than $5 with the point being a 6 or 8, single odds bets will not receive the full 6 to 5 payoff, but will be paid off at even-money only, for again, the craps tables do not stock units smaller than $1 chips.

Three Unit Bet · Single Odds Special Allowance	
Basic Three Unit Bet	**6 or 8 as Point**
$3	$5 ($6)
$15	$25 ($30)
$30	$50 ($60)
$45	$75 ($90)
$75	$125 ($150)
$300	$500 ($600)

The first column, *Basic Three Unit Bet*, indicates our standard pass and come bet. The second column shows the special allowance permitted when the point is 6 or 8. Numbers in parenthesis indicate the amount paid if the single odds bet is won. Note that this is only a partial listing of the basic three unit bets.

On bets larger than $5 but in unequal multiples of $5, the free-odds bet will be paid to the highest multiple of $5 at 6 to 5, and the remainder will be paid at even-money. Thus, a $12 odds bet on the 8 will yield a payoff of only $14, $12 on the first $10 (at 6 to 5), and even-money on the unequal remainder of $2.

When the free-odds bets do not receive their full payoff, the bet works to the player's disadvantage. Therefore, we recommend that pass and come wagers be made in multiples of $3 to allow the player to take full advantage of the special allowances and lower the house edge for the single odds game below 0.8%.

Double Odds - Pass Line

Double odds work just like single odds except that the player is allowed to bet double his pass line bet as a free-odds wager. If $10 was bet on the pass line and a 5 was established as the point, the double odds game allows the player to bet $20 as a free-odds wager and receive the same correct 3 to 2 odds on that point, instead of only being allowed a $10 free-odds bet as in the single odds game.

Special Allowances - Double Odds Game

One special allowance to keep in mind in double odds games. With a two unit bet on the pass line and the point a 6 or 8, double odds games allow the player to wager five units as a free-odds bet. Thus, with a $10 bet (two $5 unit chips), and the point a 6 or 8, a $25 double odds bet would be allowed. If won, the 6 to 5 payoff would bring $30 in winnings (six $5 chips, an easier pay-off for the casino).

We recommend that players bet in multiples of two for it permits us to take advantage of the special five unit allowance when the point is a 6 or an 8. Any bet that can be divisible by two can be considered a two unit bet and be backed by the special five unit allowance if the point is a 6 or an 8.

Two Unit Bet · Double Odds Special Allowance		
Basic Two Unit Bet	6 or 8 as Point	4, 5, 9 or 10 as Point
$2	$5 ($6)	$4
$10	$25 ($30)	$20
$20	$50 ($60)	$40
$30	$75 ($90)	$60
$50	$125 ($150)	$100
$200	$500 ($600)	$400

*The Basic Two Unit Bet is our standard pass and come bet. The third column is the normal double odds allowance for points 4, 5, 9 and 10.
Numbers in parenthesis ( ) indicate the payoff if the double odds bet is won (at 6 to 5 payoff). Other two unit bets are possible.

Free-Odds - Don't Pass

Once the point is established, don't pass bettors are allowed to make a free-odds bet that a 7 will be rolled before the point repeats. The bet is paid off at correct odds, the house enjoying no edge, and is made by placing the free-odds bet next to the don't pass wager in the don't pass box.

Don't Pass and Free-Odds Bet

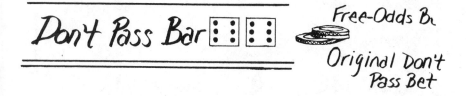

Since the odds favor the don't pass bettor once the point is established, there being more ways to roll a winning 7 than any point number, the don't pass bettor must *lay odds,* that is, put more money on the free-odds bet than he will win.

Let's say the point is a 4. The don't pass bettor's chances of winning the bet are now 2 to 1 in his favor. There are only three ways to roll a 4, a loser, against the six combinations of a 7, a winner. Therefore, the don't pass bettor must bet $20 to win $10 when the point is a 4 (or 10).

(On the other side of the bet, pass line bettors are receiving 2 to 1 odds, for their bet is the underdog, having only three winning chances against six losing combinations.)

To lay odds as a don't pass bettor, the allowable free-odds bet is determined by the *payoff*, not the original bet. Using the above example of a $10 bet on the don't pass with 4 established as the point, the don't pass bettor in a single odds game is allowed up to a $10 win on the free-odds bet.

Since the odds are 2 to 1 in his favor, the don't pass bettor must lay $20 to win $10. If it was a double odds game, meaning the player could win $20 on his original $10 bet, than at 1 to 2 odds, $40 would have to be staked for a potential win of $20.

The odds the don't pass bettor must lay are exactly opposite the odds pass line bettors take on the same points. Below is a table showing the free-odds bets from the wrong bettors position.

Like the free-odds bets for right bettors, don't pass free-odds wagers can be removed or reduced at any time, but since these are the player's best bets, it should not be done.

Odds of Rolling a Seven Before Point Repeats		
Point Number	Correct Odds	House Payoff
4 or 10	1 to 2	1 to 2
5 or 9	2 to 3	2 to 3
6 or 8	5 to 6	5 to 6

Note how the house has no percentage advantage on these bets since the payoff is identical to the correct odds.

Let's look at a quick example to see how the free-odds bet works for the don't pass bettor.

$10 is bet on the don't pass, and the ***come-out roll is a 9***. The wrong bettor ***bets $15*** behind the line as a free-odds bet, the maximum allowed in a single odds game. He stands to win $10 on the free-odds bet if the 7 is rolled before the 9 repeats, in addition to $10 on his don't pass bet.

Should the point be rolled before the 7, the $15 free-odds bet and $10 don't pass bet will be lost. If double odds were allowed, $20 would be the maximum allowable free-odds win. At 2 to 3 odds, the don't pass bettor would have to lay $30 to win $20.

Wrong Bettors Special Allowances - Single Odds

The casino makes a special provision for don't pass bettors when the point is a 5 or 9 and an odd figure such as $5 is wagered. Since the craps tables do not deal in half dollars, the player is allowed to make a free-odds bet of $9 behind the line in this instance, and if the bet is won, will get paid $6 ($9 at 2 to 3).

When the point is 5 or 9 and the original bet is unequal, the house allows the player to bet more than the straight single odds. Just ask the dealer the exact amount allowed in those instances for the rules may vary from casino to casino.

Come, Don't Come and Free-Odds Bets

Dealer will place free-odds bet atop original bet but offset to distinguish from come or don't come bet.

don't come and free-odds bet

8   *NINE*   **10**

come and free-odds bet

Free-Odds: Come and Don't Come

Once a come point is established, the bettor can take odds (or lay odds for don't come bettors) and get the same advantageous payoffs, 2-1 on points 4 and 10 (1-2 for wrong bettors), 3-2 on the 5 and 9 (2-3), and 6-5 on the 6 and 8 (5-6). The same special allowances apply for these free-odds bets.

The house has no advantage on these wagers, and like the line bets, the overall house edge on the come or don't come bets teamed with single odds drops to 0.8%, and with double odds, to 0.6%.

However, the odds bets on the come and don't come bets are placed differently than line bets. Rather than being made by the player, the odds bets are given to the dealer to place with the instruction, "odds on the come," or "odds on the don't come."

The dealer will place the odds bet in the appropriate box atop the come point, but slightly offset, so that the odds bet can be differentiated from the come bet.

The only other difference is with the come bet. While the come bet itself is working on the come-out roll, the odds bet on that come bet is not. Let's say the player had $15 bet on the come point of 6 and had that bet backed by $25 free-odds. A come-out roll of a 7 would of course be a loser for the $15 come bet, as that bet is always working, but since the free-odds bet was off, the $25 single odds wager would be returned to the player.

If a 6 was rolled instead, a winner for the come bet, the player would only win the $15, and be returned the $25 odds bet.

Though it is standard procedure for the free-odds bet backing the come wager to be off on the come-out roll, the player can request the odds bet to be "on" by informing the dealer that the "odds are on for the come bet," and then, of course, the odds bet is subject to the normal rules.

The odds on the don't come bets, as with the pass and don't pass wagers, are always working.

THE REST OF THE BETS

With the exception of the place bet of 6 and 8, none of the bets presented in this section, which include the remainder of the bets possible at craps, are recommended for play. The house edge over the player on these bets is too large to be incorporated into a winning strategy, and the bettor making these bets will soon find himself drained of significant portions of his bankroll.

The bets listed in this section are discussed anyway so that the player has a full understanding of all the bets possible at craps, and so that the player is never tempted to make these poor wagers.

Place Bets

The **place bets** are among the most popular wagers in craps, and are a bet that a particular point number, whichever is wagered on, the 4, 5, 6, 8, 9 or 10, is rolled before a 7 is thrown. The player can make as many place bets as he wants, and some players do, covering all the numbers with place bets.

However, this is not recommended strategy, for as we will see, with the exception of the place bets of 6 and 8, the other place bets, the 4, 5, 9 and 10, are poor wagers, and will have no role in our winning strategies.

Place bets are made by giving the dealer the desired wager, and telling him, for example, "to place the 9," or any such statement that indicates the player wants to make a place bet on the 9.

Though place bets can be made at any time, they are not working, or are "**off**" on the come-out roll, unless the player requests them to be "**on**" (working). The player can also request his place bets to be off for a limited series of throws, and may increase, reduce or remove them at any time prior to a roll.

House Payoffs on Place Bets			
Bet	**Payoff**	**Correct Odds**	**House Edge**
4 or 10	9 to 5	2 to 1	6.67%
5 or 9	7 to 5	3 to 2	4.00%
6 or 8	7 to 6	6 to 5	1.52%

To get the full payoffs on the place bets, the player should make his bets in the proper multiples. On place bets of 4 and 10, and 5 and 9, the bets should be made in multiples of $5 since the payoffs are 9 to 5 and 7 to 5 respectively. On the 6 and 8, the bet should be in multiples of $6 (7 to 6 payoff).

Excess bets in unequal multiples will be paid off at even-money only and work to the player's disadvantage. For example, a $10 bet on the 6 will be paid as follows: The first $6 will get the full 7 to 6 odds for $7, while the remaining $4 gets paid at even-money, or $4, for a total $11 win. The last $4, paid at only even-money, is a terrible payoff, and makes the entire bet a poor one.

Unless the player makes the place bets of 6 or 8 in multiples of $6 to insure full payoffs, the bet should not be made. Also, bets less than $5 on the 4, 5, 9 and 10, and less than $6 on the 6 and 8, will be paid of at only even-money.

To summarize, do not make place bets of 4 or 10, or 5 and 9, for the house edge is too high.

The place bets of 6 and 8 have playable odds of 1.52% and can be used in an aggressive maximize gain strategy, though some players may prefer to stick with the line, come and don't come bets backed by free-odds, the best bets of all.

Big 6 and Big 8

The **Big 6** and **Big 8** are bets that a particular number bet on, the 6 or 8, is thrown before a 7 is rolled. These bets can be made at any time, and are bet by putting the wager into the box marked Big 6 or Big 8.

These bets work just like the place bets of 6 and 8 except that the house only pays even-money on a won bet as opposed to the 7 to 6 payoff he would receive had he made the superior place bet on 6 or 8 instead. The house has a whopping 9.90% advantage on the Big 6 and Big 8 bets.

Buying the 4 or 10

This is an option the casino gives the player when betting on a place number, and though it reduces the odds on the 4 or 10 from 6.67% to 4.76%, the buy bet is still a poor one and should not be made. But here's how it works.

To **buy** the 4 or 10, you must give the house a 5% commission on your bet. Once you've bought a number, the house will pay off the bet at the correct odds. Thus, your payoff will be 2 to 1, the correct odds, rather than 9 to 5 as is usually the payoff for these place bets.

A 5% commission on $20 would be $1. For any bet smaller than $20, the commission would still be $1 since the craps tables generally carry no smaller units. In these cases, the house edge on your buy bet would be much larger than 4.76%. If you buy the 4

112

and 10 at $10 each, for a total of $20, the commission would only be 5% of the two bet total, or $1.

Like the place bets, buy bets are not working on the come-out roll, unless you instruct the dealer that the bet is on. They are also similar to the place bets in that they can be increased, reduced or removed at any time prior to the roll. Note that an increased buy bet is subject to the 5% commission on the additional wager.

Some casinos will keep the 5% commission if you decide to remove an established bet or charge an additional 5% if you win your bet and decide to let it ride.

Buying the 5, 6, 8, 9

Theoretically, you can buy these numbers as well, but since the commission is 5%, and the house edge on all these place bets is less than that, there is no advantage in buying these numbers.

Lay Bets

The **lay bet** is the opposite of a buy bet, and is used by wrong bettors who are wagering that the 7 will be thrown before the point or points they bet against is rolled. While the bet is paid off at correct odds, it costs the bettor 5% commission on the projected win to get this payoff, and is therefore, a poor bet.

Lay bets, which can be bet added to, reduced or removed altogether at any time, are made by giving the dealer your chips along with the required 5% commission on the projected win. The dealer will place the bet above the point number covered (in the area where the don't come bets are placed) and place a buy button on top to distinguish the lay bet.

To receive the full value on the lay bet of 4 or 10, the bettor would have to wager at least $40 to win $20 (1 to 2 odds). The 5% commission on the projected win of $20 would be $1. Any bet smaller than the $40 lay bet on the 4 or 10 would still be charged the minimum $1 commission (craps tables do not generally deal in currency smaller than $1 chips) making the house edge greater than the 2.44% advantage already built into this wager.

The 5 and 9 lay bets would require a minimum wager of $30 for the player to get the maximum value. The potential $20 win (laying odds at 2 to 3) would be charged $1 commission. The 6 and 8 bets would require a wager of $24 at 5 to 6 odds on a projected win of $20 to get full value from the commission. Any bet smaller than the projected win of $20 would still be charged the minimum $1 commission, and raise the overall house edge on the wager.

House Allowance on Lay Bets	
Points	House Advantage
4 or 10	2.44%
5 or 9	3.23%
6 or 8	4.00%

Field Bet

The **field bet** is a one roll wager that the next throw of the dice will be a number listed in the field box, the 2, 3, 4, 9, 10, 11 or 12. If one of the numbers not listed is rolled, the 5, 6, 7 or 8, then the bet is lost.

The field bet can be made at any time and is done by placing the wager in the area marked "Field".

At first glance, the bet seems attractive. There are seven winning numbers listed in the field box, and two of these numbers, the 2 and the 12, pay double if they are rolled. In some casinos, the 2 or 12 pays triple. The other winning numbers, the 3, 4, 9, 10 and 11 pay even-money. However, there are 20 combinations (of the 5, 6, 7 and 8) that will beat us, and only 16 that will win, giving the house an edge of 5.55% when the 2 and 12 are paid at 2 to 1, and 2.7% when one is paid at 2 to 1 and the other at 3 to 1.

Proposition, or Center Bets

The **proposition**, or **center bets**, as they are sometimes called, are located at the center of the layout, and are made by either giving the chips to the dealer who will pass them along to the stickman, or, as with the hardways bet or craps-eleven bet, can sometimes be tossed directly to the stickman.

The central area of the layout is under the complete domain of the stickman, and though he will physically handle the placing and removing of bets in this area, it is with the dealer that the player will generally make his bets and receive his payoffs.

The proposition bets are the worst bets a player can make at craps and should never be made. The house advantage rages as high as 16.67% on some of these wagers. However, these bets are listed and their odds explained so that the reader will be fully conversant with all the wagers possible at craps.

Any Seven

This bet that the following roll of the dice will be a 7, is paid off by the house at 4 to 1 (5 for 1), and is among the worst bets a player can make. The house maintains an exorbitant edge of 16.67% over the player. Don't even make this bet in your dreams.

Any Craps

This bet, located at the bottom of the center layout and along its sides, is a bet that the following roll will be a craps - a 2, 3 or 12.

There are four ways to roll a winner. The 2 and 12 account for one way each, while there are two ways to roll a three. The other 32 combinations are losers, making the correct odds 8 to 1. The house only pays 7 to 1, giving them an 11.1% advantage.

2 or 12

This is a bet that the next roll of the dice will come up a 2, or a 12 if you bet that number, and is paid off by the house at 30 to 1. Of the 36 possible combinations of the dice, there is only one way of rolling a 2 or a 12, making the correct odds 35 to 1 against rolling either number. With only a 30 to 1 payoff, the house enjoys a hefty 13.69% advantage.

Sometimes a casino may only pay off at 30 for 1 (29 to 1), giving them an edge of 16.67%. This should make no difference to us for we won't go near that bet in either case.

3 or 11

This is a wager that the following roll will be a 3, or an 11, whichever you place your money on, and the house payoff is 15 to 1. Since there are only 2 ways to roll either number out of a possible 36 combinations, the correct odds are 17 to 1 (34 losers, 2 winners). The house edge is 11.1%. Where the payoff is 15 for 1 (14 to 1), this edge jumps to 16.67%.

Horn Bet

It takes four chips or multiples thereof to makes this bet. The horn bet is a four way bet that the next roll will be a 2, 3, 11 or 12, in effect combining four poor bets together. The house pays off the winning number at the normal payoffs (15 to 1 for the 3 or 11, and 30 to 1 for the 2 or 12), and deducts the other three losing chips from the payoff.

This sucker bet combines four losing wagers for a combined house edge of 11.1%, or 16.67% with the poorer payoffs discussed earlier. Never make this bet.

Hop Bet

This one roll wager, which does not appear on the layout, is generally made on a combination of the dice not otherwise offered on the one roll bets, such as 2, 3. If the bet is a pair such as 5, 5, the player will get the same payoff as the casino gives on the 2 or 12 bet (30 to 1 or 29 to 1). If the bet is a non-pair, such as 4, 5, which has two ways to win (4, 5; 5, 4), the payoff will be the same as on the 3 or 11 bet (15 to 1 or 14 to 1).

To make a hop bet, give your bet to the dealer or stickman, and call out for example "Hop 54", if the 5, 4 is the hop bet you wish to make. With the more generous payoff hop bets give the casino an edge of 13.39%, otherwise the edge is 16.67%. In either case, consider the bet a donation to the casino.

Craps-Eleven

The stickman will constantly exhort the player to make this horrendous bet, which is an appeal to bet the Any Craps and 11 bet simultaneously. We don't want to go near either bet by itself let alone together. Save your money for the show.

Hardways

Whenever the numbers, 4, 6, 8 or 10 are rolled as doubles, the roll is said to be thrown **hardways**. A throw of 2-2 is said to be **4, the hardway** or **hard 4**, and similarly with 3-3, 4-4 and 5-5 for hard 6, 8 and 10 respectively. Rolling the 4, 6, 8 and 10 in other combinations is called **easy** such as 6-4; **10 the easy way**.

Betting hardways is betting that the particular number you choose comes up hard before it comes up easy or before a 7 is thrown.

Hard 4 and Hard 10

There is only one way to throw a hard 4 (2-2) or hard 10 (5-5), and eight ways to lose - six ways to roll a seven, and two ways to throw a 4 or 10 the easy way (1-3, 3-1, 6-4 and 4-6). The correct odds are 8 to 1 but the house only pays 7 to 1 for an advantage of 11.1%. This weak bet should never be made.

Hard 6 and Hard 8

There are a total of 10 losing combinations - the 6 ways to roll a 7, and 4 ways to roll a 6 or an 8 the easy way. There is only 1 way to throw the 6 or 8 the hardway. The correct odds of this hardway bet is 10 to 1 but the house only pays 9 to 1, a hefty 9.09% edge.

WINNING STRATEGIES:
BETTING WITH THE DICE

We'll use only the best bets in our strategies - the pass line, come and free-odds wagers, wagers which give the player the best chances of winning, and lower the house edge to 0.8% in single odds games and 0.6% in double odds ones.

Built-in to the strategies are methods to turn average wins into big winning sessions without any risk of big losses.

Basic Conservative Method - Single Odds Strategy

Our standard bet will be in increments of three units so that we can take advantage of the special free-odds allowances should the points be 6 or 8, whereupon we can back our pass line or come bet by five units, or points 5 or 9, where we can bet extra if the original bet is uneven such as $15, where $20 would be permitted as a free-odds wager.

This allows maximum usage of the free-odds bets, wagers the house has no edge on, and brings the overall house advantage down to the barest minimum possible in a single odds game.

These are the guidelines of the **Basic Conservative Strategy:**

1. We will make three unit pass line and come bets until we have two points established, and back both those bets with the maximum single odds allowed.

2. Every time a point repeats, whether as a come or pass line point, we will make another three unit pass line or come bet so that we continue to have two points working for us. If a 2, 3, 11 or 12 declares a winner or a loser on the new pass line or come bet, we will follow with another bet until we get that second point established and then take the maximum single odds allowed on that point.

3. If the shooter sevens-out, clearing the board of all bets, we'll begin the progression again with a new pass line bet.

Aggressive Method - Single Odds Strategy

Rather than playing only two points as in the **Basic Conservative Strategy**, this method immediately attempts to establish three points. Otherwise, all the principles and methods are the same.

With three points covered, the bettor using the **Aggressive Strategy** can make a lot of money when the shooter starts rolling numbers.

Double Odds Strategies

Whenever the bettor has a choice, he should always choose a double odds game over a single odds game, for the additional allowance of the free-odds bet drops the overall house edge from 0.8% to 0.6% when using our methods.

The playing strategies we will pursue in the double odds game are identical to the single odds game except that we will bet in units of two instead of units of three as recommended in the single odds game to take advantage of the special five unit free-odds allowance when the point is 6 or 8.

Basic Conservative Strategy bettors should establish two points with maximum double odds, while **Aggressive Strategy** bettors will want to cover three points. Follow the procedures for the single odds methods substituting only the two unit basic bet for the three unit bet, and making double odds bets instead of single odds.

Maximizing Profits - Double Odds Game

Again our strategy here will follow that of the single odds game except we'll be increasing our bets by two units instead of three.

Basic Conservative Strategy bettors won't begin increasing bets until they've accumulated 20 units in profits, and Aggressive bettors will need 25 units. Remember to take advantage of the special allowances when the point is a 6 or 8. A four unit bet can be backed by 10 units in the double odds game, and a six unit bet by 15.

When eventually the shooter sevens-out, ending our winning streak, we'll start the next progression again at two units, ready to capitalize on another hot roll should one develop.

WINNING STRATEGIES: BETTING AGAINST THE DICE

Though the odds of winning are equivalent to the right betting strategies, 0.8% in a single odds game and 0.6% in a double odds game, very few craps players bet against the dice. Many bettors feel uncomfortable about having to *lay odds*, putting more money on their free-odds bet than they'll win, but as stated earlier, the free-odds wagers give the house no edge betting right or wrong.

However, players betting against the dice don't mind laying odds, for the roll of a 7, their winner, will occur more often than any point number, and they'll have frequent winners.

In addition, should a point be repeated, a losing roll for wrong bettors, only one bet will be lost. The other points covered by the wrong bettor are still in play. On the other side of the dice, the right bettors fear the 7, for when it is thrown - boom - all their established points and free-odds bets are lost.

We will apply the same principles of play as right bettors. We'll make only the best bets available to us, those that reduce the house edge to the lowest possible figure - the don't pass, the don't come and free-odds bets.

Basic Conservative Method - Wrong Bettors
Single Odds Strategy

Our standard bet will be in even increments of two units. Bets such as $15 or $25 are difficult to work with when the point is a 5 or 9 and 2 to 3 odds should be laid. Betting in other unit sizes is equally valid, but the player will find it easiest to work in multiples of $10.

These are the guidelines of the **Basic Conservative Strategy:**

1. We will make two unit don't pass and don't come bets until we have established bets against two points, and back both those bets with maximum free-odds.

2. Should a point repeat, a loser for us, we will make another don't come or don't pass bet, so that we can continue to have bets working against two points. If a 2, 3, 11 or 12 determines a winner or loser on a new don't pass or don't come bet, we will follow with another bet until we get that second point established, and then we'll play the maximum single odds against that point.

3. Stop establishing don't pass and don't come bets if a second point repeats. This is an important safeguard to protect us against bad losing streaks.

4. If a 7 is thrown, a winner on all our bets, we'll begin the progression again with our two unit don't pass bet.

As cautious bettors, we'll limit ourselves to only two points and strictly follow the safeguards recommended in step 3.

Aggressive Method - Wrong Bettors
Single Odds Strategy

Our **Aggressive Strategy** follows the same guidelines as the **Basic-Conservative Strategy** except that we'll cover three points during a shoot instead of two, and will stop making additional don't pass and don't come bets if three points repeat, instead of two as advised in the **Basic Conservative Strategy**.

We'll use the same bets - the don't pass, don't come and free-odds bets, and enjoy the same low 0.8% house edge as in a single odds game.

Double Odds Strategy - Wrong Bettors

Whenever possible, the wrong bettor should play a double odds game over a single odds game, for it lowers the overall house edge from 0.8% to 0.6%.

And we always want to play with the best odds we can get - the lower the house edge, the greater our chances of winning.

By nature, the double odds strategies are more aggressive than the single odds games, and are more in tune for players whose temperament demands hotter action. The double odds bettor lays more to win more and therefore needs a larger bankroll than his single odds counterpart. Therefore, to play this strategy, the double odds bettor must feel comfortable with the larger bet levels.

Our double odds strategies are identical to the single odds methods, except that we're playing double odds instead of single odds. We'll begin by making a two unit don't pass bet, and backing that bet by double odds once a point is established.

Basic Conservative Strategy bettors will follow with a don't come bet and lay double odds on both points while **Aggressive Strategy** bettors will make two more don't come bets backed by the full double odds.

Like the single odds strategies, **Basic Conservative Strategy** players attempt to keep two points working at all times while

Aggressive Strategy players strive for three working points.

When points repeat, new don't pass or don't come bets are made to reestablish another point, but should a second point repeat for **Basic Conservative Strategy** players or a third point for **Aggressive Strategy** players, then we'll curtail all new betting until the shooter sevens-out, a winner on our remaining bets.

We employ this stop-loss as a safeguard to protect against one really bad shoot wiping out our table stakes. However, should the dice start blowing profits in our direction, we're immediately ready to capitalize on the situation.

We start the next come-out roll fresh, with a two unit don't pass wager, always ready for the streak that will mint chips for us.

BECOMING A BETTER CRAPS PLAYER

Serious craps players that want to take a run at the casinos money may want to use the professional strategies of the Cardoza Craps Master. These advanced strategies show players how to win money from hot, cold and choppy tables. See back pages for more information.

PLAYING KENO TO WIN

INTRODUCTION

The origins of this fun game go back some 2,000 years to the Han Dynasty in China - quite a long history, and quite a long distance to travel to make it to casinos as far away as Nevada, halfway across the globe.

Keno is quite popular and one of the attractions of the game is that it's easy to play. The only decisions a player need be concerned with are which numbers he or she will play, and how much to bet. Once the bet is placed, the fun begins as number upon number appear on the board, and the player waits to see if indeed, enough lucky numbers were hit to bring in the big fish.

And there's always that attraction of the giant win - that a 70¢ or $1.00 or $1.40 wager, whatever is played, may catch the right numbers and land the lucky bettor a $50,000 bonanza.

Let's move on now, see how the game is played, and how best to make yourself a winner.

THE BASICS OF KENO

All bets in keno are made and recorded on a **keno ticket**, a pre-printed form where a player indicates the choices he or she will make. The tickets are readily available in the keno lounge and are kept in generous supply on the counters and next to every seat in the keno area.

Situated near the tickets will be the thick, black crayons which are used to mark keno tickets, and the casinos rate card, showing the exact payoffs for tickets played and won.

There are 80 numbered squares on a keno ticket which correspond exactly to the 80 numbered balls in the keno cage. A player may choose anywhere from one to fifteen numbers to play, and does so by marking an "x" on the keno ticket for each number or numbers he or she so chooses.

You'll notice on the keno ticket, "KENO LIMIT $50,000, To aggregate players each game." This means that if you do hit the big $50,000 prize in the same game as another player, that you'll have to split the jackpot. However, the likelihood of this occurring stretches the imagination into far off places - in other words - don't worry about it.

Twenty balls will be drawn each game, and will appear as lighted numbers on the keno screens. As the game progresses, each number will be lit as it is drawn, so that the player can easily keep track of the numbers drawn and see how his or her ticket is faring.

Winnings are determined by consulting the payoff chart each casino provides. If enough numbers have been correctly picked, you have a winner, and the chart will show the payoff. The more numbers that come up, the greater the winnings.

Betting

Bets are usually made in 70¢ or $1.00 multiples, though other standard bets may apply. A player may bet as many multiples of this bet as he desires. For example, a player may bet $5.00 on a $1.00 ticket, giving him or her in fact, five games with the same combinations.

How to Mark the Ticket

The amount being wagered on a game should be placed in the box marked Mark Price Here in the upper right hand corner of the ticket. Leave out dollar or cents signs though. $1 would be indicated by simply placing 1- and 70 cents by .70-. Of course, any amount up to the house limit can be wagered.

Underneath this box is a column of white space. The number of spots selected for the game is put here. If six spots were selected on the ticket, mark the number 6, if fifteen numbers, mark 15.

Let's show a five spot ticket that we've marked for a $1 game.

Five Spot Ticket

1	2	3	4	✗	6	7	8	9	10
11	✗	13	14	15	16	17	18	19	20
21	22	23	24	25	26	27	✗	29	30
31	32	33	34	35	36	37	38	39	40

KENO LIMIT $50,000.00 TO AGGREGATE PLAYERS EACH GAME

41	42	43	44	45	46	47	48	49	50
51	52	53	54	✗	56	57	58	59	60
61	✗	63	64	65	66	67	68	69	70
71	72	73	74	75	76	77	78	79	80

KENO RUNNERS ARE AVAILABLE FOR YOUR CONVENIENCE
WE ARE NOT RESPONSIBLE IF TICKETS ARE TOO LATE FOR CURRENT GAME

This type of ticket, which is the most common one bet, is called a straight ticket, or more precisely, in this example, a five-spot straight ticket. Similarly, if 11 numbers were chosen, it would be called an 11 spot straight ticket.

The Duplicate Ticket

Now you have your ticket filled in and are ready to play the game. You take this original or master ticket to the keno writer at the window and hand it in with the $ amount for which you'll be playing. The writer will retain your original ticket and hand back a duplicate ticket. This ticket will show the same numbers you have chosen, which are generally marked in thick black strokes from the brush they use, the dollar amount of the game and the total numbers played, just like your ticket did.

It will also show some things that were not on your original. The duplicate will have printed on it, the date and time of the game, the game's number, and a particular code number used by the casino. You'll also see the printing, "Winning tickets must be paid immediately after each keno game," or some such writing.

Take this piece of writing very seriously. If you have a winning ticket, you must present your duplicate before the next game resumes, or you will forfeit that payoff.

125

The Keno Runner

Many casinos offer players the luxury of playing keno from virtually anywhere in the casino. One can play the game while at the slots or while luxuriating over a meal in the restaurant.

This is done through the services of a keno runner, casino employees, usually women, whose sole job is to take keno bets from patrons in various parts of the casino, return to them a duplicate ticket and collect their payoff should the ticket be a winner.

Ah, the easy life! If you do win, it is customary to tip a little something to the runner (the bearer of good tidings).

Replaying A Ticket

You may have a lucky set of numbers you like to play, or a particular set that either just won for you, or which you've just played, and feel that the same numbers are ripe to score.

In any case, the casino allows you to replay the same numbers again, and to save you the trouble of rewriting your ticket, you simply need to hand in your duplicate, which now becomes your original ticket, and the keno writer will issue you a new duplicate.

Easy as that. You can do this all day long if you like, exchanging duplicate as original for a new duplicate.

Other Tickets

Players are not limited to just straight tickets but may also play as many combinations as they choose. There are split, combination, way, and king tickets. We recommend you buy David Cowles' Complete Guide to Winning Keno and his powerful advanced strategy, the GRI Master Keno Strategy, to learn more about these tickets.

Special Tickets

Casinos often promote their keno games in various ways, perhaps through a coupon or special incentive, and in many of these instances they'll present the player with a special ticket - a keno ticket that must be played a certain way and that will pay according to a different payoff structure - marked on the special payoff chart you will receive.

These tickets generally offer the player a little better deal than the regular ticket and are an incentive to get him or her to play a game, for generally speaking, it's difficult to play just one game. However, do check the payoff rate to make sure that indeed the payoff is more attractive than the regular card.

When playing a special card, make sure you indicate this on your ticket by marking "SP" for special on your original ticket, or otherwise following the instructions on the special ticket sheet.

WINNING STRATEGY

Keno is a game that should not be played seriously for the odds are prohibitively against the player. The house edge is typically well over 20% and can be as high as 35% - daunting odds if one wants to win in the long run. There are ways, shown in GRI Master Keno Strategy, to cut down these odds, and in special instances, when there's a keno promotion, to actually get an edge.

One thing to look out for is that some casinos offer better payoffs on the big win than others so a little shopping might get you closer to a bigger payoff. And if you find a casino offering $50,000 or higher on a big win as opposed to $25,000 or whatever for the same number of spots hit, by all means, play for the bigger total.

Keno is a great game to test out your lucky numbers. Picking birth dates, anniversaries, license plate numbers and the like offer a big pool of possibilities to see which ones will really pay off.

Perhaps you like the evens, odds and doubles as used in one of our examples, or a progression using every fourth number, or numbers having either a 3 or a 5 in it.

Do you play the same numbers and combinations every game or switch around when one set fails? And what if the original set then wins, or if you didn't switch and the numbers you would have played won? Oh, the heartaches!

If you know your lucky numbers, you may just give them a whirl and see if you can't walk away with a $50,000 bonanza!

PLAYING ROULETTE TO WIN

INTRODUCTION

Roulette offers player a huge variety of bets, more than any other casino table game, and the constant possibilities of winning and the different payoffs of the wagers, ranging from even-money payoffs to returns of 35 to 1, keeps the game exciting and suspenseful.

We'll show you how to make all the different bets possible in roulette, the odds involved and how the game is played both here and abroad so that you'll be ready to play roulette anywhere in the world and be fully prepared to win!

THE BASICS OF ROULETTE

The Roulette Setting

Roulette is played with a circular wheel containing 36 grooved slots numbered from 1 to 36, half the numbers of which are black and the other half red, a tiny ball which is used in conjunction with the wheel, and a betting layout where players can place their wagers.

In addition to the 36 numbers on the roulette wheel, the American game has a 0 and 00, while the European game has but one 0. The zero slots are neither red nor black as are the other numbers but are green in color.

The wheel is cut into tiny pockets, one for each number - 37 total on a European wheel and 38 on an American - so that the ball, when spun around the wheel, will eventually fall into one of these slots - that number being the winning spin.

The European game generally has the wheel flanked on two sides by a betting layout, so that the busy tables can accommodate players on both sides of the wheel, while the less popular American games typically use but one layout to the side.

The Layout

00	3	6	9	12	15	18	21	24	27	30	33	36	2-1
	2	5	8	11	14	17	20	23	26	29	32	35	2-1
0	1	4	7	10	13	16	19	22	25	28	31	34	2-1

1st 12			2nd 12			3rd 12		
1to18	EVEN	◇		◆		ODD	19to36	

The Dealer

The American game typically employs just one dealer who handles all of the functions at the table. He changes money into chips, spins the wheel, collects losing bets and pays off the winners. In between he finds time to stack and restack collected chips from the layout into neat, colorful piles, so that payoffs from the next spin will proceed smoothly and rapidly.

If a table is exceptionally busy, the dealer may have an assistant to help run the game.

European style games have one to as many as three or four **croupiers**, the French term for dealers, paying and collecting bets on the two adjacent layouts, and a **tourneur**, whose main responsibility is to spin the wheel and call the result. Often, a supervisor will be present as well.

129

Thus, when things get rolling and the tables crowded, one might find as many as six casino personnel manning a roulette game - a tourneur, four croupiers and a supervisor.

The Play of the Game

Once players have placed their bets on the layout, choosing from the myriad possibilities available in front of them, the game is officially ready to begin. The roulette wheel will be spun by the dealer or tourneur who immediately afterwards, will throw the ball in the opposite direction from which the wheel is spinning so that both ball and wheel are racing in opposite directions on the wheel itself.

Players must now get in their last minute wagers for when the ball is about to leave the track, the dealer will announce that bets are no longer permitted. The call of *Faites vos jeux, messieurs* (Make your bets gentlemen) or *Rien ne va plus* (Nothing more goes) are classic in the French speaking casinos.

When the ball stops, the dealer or tourneur will call out the outcome, and a marker will be placed on the number just spun so that all players and dealers can clearly see the winning number.

The dealers or **croupiers**, as they're called in French, will now settle the wagers. Lost bets are collected first by the dealers, and after this is done, all the winning bets will be paid off.

The Chips

Keeping track of one's bets are easy in American roulette games, for each player is issued special chips applicable only to the roulette game at that casino, and these chips are colored, a different color for each player. Ten different players may be represented by, for example, yellow, red, pink, blue, green, black, white, beige, purple and grey chips.

The colored chips are valid and can be used only at the roulette table which issues them. If the table is crowded and no more colors are available, a player may use regular casino chips for his or her bets.

There is no confusion in ownership of the chips this way. Color coding makes life easy at these tables. When a player approaches the roulette table, he exchanges cash or casino chips for an equivalent value in the colored chips, called in the parlance of the game, **wheel checks**. The value assigned to those colored chips, be it 25¢, $1.00, $5.00 or whatever, is set by the player. Thus, if the player wants to value the chips at 25¢, more chips will be issued from the dealer than if the chips were valued at $1.00.

The dealer will place a coin or **marker button** on top of the colored chips and place these on the stationary outer rim of the wheel, so that the value of that wheel check is clearly marked.

When a player is ready to leave, he converts the wheel checks back into the regular casino checks with the dealer at that table.

Life is a bit more complicated in the European style game where color coding is not used and bettors simply use casino chips or cash to make their bets. Sometimes, in the confusion of a crowded game, vociferous arguments ensue as players lay identical claim to chips on the felt.

The Basic Odds

The primary difference in the popularity of European and American roulette lies in the simple fact that the European game gives the player much better odds of winning, and this is where the 0, 00 difference of the two wheels comes into play.

Let's see how the odds are figured.

There are slots numbered from 1 to 36 on the roulette wheel - a total of 36. There is only one way to win for each number chosen. That leaves 35 other numbers, which if they come up, are losers for the bettor. True odds of 35 to 1 against - 35 ways to lose, one way to win.

And that exactly what the casino will pay on a single number bet. So where is the casino's profit?

It is the zeros added to the wheel that give casinos their edge, for now there are a total of 37 possibilities on a European wheel (single zero added) and 38 possibilities on an American one (double zero added). The casino's payoff is still 35 to 1, being based on the true odds of a 36 number wheel. However, with the added zeros, the true odds on a single number bet are now 36 to 1 on a single zero wheel (the European game) and 37 to 1 on a double zero wheel (the American game).

Those zeros give the casino its edge on all bets made. Unless the zero (and in American roulette the 00 also) are bet directly, the spin of either on the wheel causes all other wagers to lose.

The sole exceptions are the even-money bets in a European style game (and Atlantic City), for the spin of a zero gives the red-black (rouge-noir), high-low (passe-manque) and odd-even (impair-pair) bettors a second chance, and reduces the house edge on these bets to 1.35% (2.63% in Atlantic City) - the best odds one can receive in roulette.

The zeros represent the house advantage and that is why the 00 in American roulette makes that game a worse gamble for the player than its European counterpart. Atlantic City makes up for this a little by offering surrender on even-money bets, bringing the casino's edge on these wagers down to 2.63%.

Let's sum up the odds for you in chart form so that you can clearly see them in one spot.

Casino Edge in Roulette	
American Roulette (Double Zero)	**House Edge**
The 5-Number Bet	7.89%
All Other Bets	5.26%
Atlantic City - Even Money Bets	2.63%
European Roulette (One Zero)	
Even-Money Bets - En Prison Rule	1.35%
All Other Bets	2.70%

The difference between the 1.35% of European style roulette and 5.26% of the American style is significant, almost a four-fold increase, which calculates directly to a loss rate four times as fast.

Now you can see why roulette with a single zero and en

prison rule is the rage of Europe, and double zero American roulette is less popular.

THE BETS

Roulette offers the player a multitude of possible wagers, more than any other casino table game. All in all, there are over 150 possible combinations to bet. And a player may make as many bets in whatever combinations desired as long as the bets fit within the minimum and maximum limit of the casino.

Let's now examine the bets one by one. (The French terms for the bets are listed in the parenthesis.)

Combination or Inside Bets

These bets are made within the numbers on the layout, and hence, are termed **inside bets**.

Single Number Bet - (En Plein)

A **single number bet** can be made on any number on the layout including the 0 and 00. To make this wager, place your chip within the lines of the number chosen, being careful not to touch the lines. Otherwise you may have another bet altogether.

The winning payoff is 35 to 1.

The Single Number Bet

Split Bet (A Cheval)

Place the chip on the line adjoining two numbers. If either number comes up, the payoff is 17 to 1.

Split Bet (A Cheval)

4	5	6
7	8	9

Trio Bet (Transversale)

The chip is placed on the outside vertical line alongside any line of numbers. If any of the three are hit, the payoff is 11 to 1.

Trio Bet (Transversale)

4-Number Bet (Carre)

Also called a square or corner bet. Place the chip on the spot marking the intersection of four numbers. If any of the four come in it is an 8 to 1 payoff.

4-Number Bet (Carre)

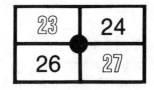

Quatre Premiere

Only in European roulette. The bet covering the 0, 1, 2 and 3. An 8 to 1 payoff.

5-Number Bet

Only in American roulette. Place the chip at the intersection of the 0, 00 and 2 to cover those numbers plus the 1 and 3. If any of these five come home, the payoff is 6 to 1. In American roulette, it is the only bet not giving the house an edge of 5.26%. It's worse - 7.89%!

5-Number Bet

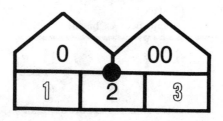

6-Number Bet (Sixaine)

Also called a **block bet**. The chip should be put on the outside line of the layout while intersecting the line separating the sets of numbers chosen. The payoff is 5 to 1.

6-Number Bet (Sixaine)

28	29	30
31	32	33

Outside Bets

These bets are outside the 36 numbers on the layout, and are aptly called, the outside bets. These include the columns, dozens and even money bets - red-black, high-low and odd-even.

Outside Bets

1st 12	2nd 12	3rd 12		
1to18	EVEN ◇	◆	ODD	19to36

Columns Bet (Colonne)

A chip placed at the head of a column, on the far side from the zero or zeros, covers all 12 numbers in the column and has a winning payoff of 2 to 1.

The 0 and 00 are not included in this bet and would be a loser if they come up.

Columns Bet (Colonne)

3	6	9	12	15	18	21	24	27	30	33	36	2-1
2	5	8	11	14	17	20	23	26	29	32	35	2-1
1	4	7	10	13	16	19	22	25	28	31	34	2-1

Dozens Bet (Douzaine)

This is another way to bet 12 numbers, either numbers 1 to 12, 13 to 24 or 25 to 36. On the American layout they're called the **first**, **second** and **third dozen** respectively, and on the French layout, they're known as **P12**, **M12** and **D12**. The winning payoff as in the column bet is 2 to 1.

Dozens Bet (Douzaine)

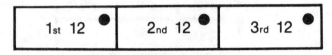

Even-Money Bets

There is one final type of bet, the even money bets: Red-Black (Rouge-Noir), High - Low (Passe-Manque) and Odd-Even (Impair-Pair). Spots for these bets are found outside the numbers, thus classified as *outside wagers*.

These wagers are clearly marked in large boxes.

In Atlantic City and European style roulette, these are the best at the roulette table, for they offer the player additional features which are greatly advantageous to the player. In Europe, the features are called en prison and partage, and in Atlantic City, surrender.

First we'll go over the bets, and after, we'll examine how the en prison, partage and surrender rules work and how they affect the player.

Even-Money Bets

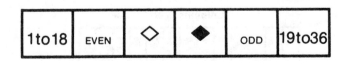

Red-Black (Rouge-Noir)

There are 18 black and eighteen red numbers. A player may bet either the **red** or the **black** and is paid off at 1 to 1 on a winning spin.

Red-Black (Rouge-Noir)

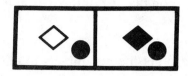

High-Low (Passe-Manque)

Numbers 1-18 may be bet (**low**) or 19-36 (**high**). Bets are paid off at 1 to 1.

High-Low (Passe-Manque)

Odd-Even (Impair-Pair)

A player may bet on the 18 even numbers (**even**) or on the 18 odd numbers (**odd**). Winning bets are paid at 1 to 1.

Odd-Even (Impair-Pair)

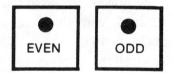

En Prison and Partage

It is on these even number bets - Red-Black, High-Low and Odd-Even - where the American and European games really differ. In American roulette, the house automatically wins on these bets when the 0 or 00 is spun (except in Atlantic City). However, in Europe, if the 0 is spun, the **en prison** rule comes into effect. The player has two choices now.

He or she can either surrender half the bet, called **partage**, or elect to allow the bet to be "imprisoned" one more spin. If the spin is won, the bet stays intact and is "released" for the player to do what he or she will. If the spin is lost, so is the bet.

This rule is greatly advantageous to the player, and brings the odds down on these bets to 1.35% in favor of the casino as opposed to the 2.70% on the rest of the bets in the single zero game.

Surrender

In an attempt to get more gamblers to play roulette, the game in Atlantic City helps make up for the 00 of the American wheel by offering **surrender**, which is really partage by another name. When a 0 or 00 is spun, players with bets on any of the even-money propositions lose only half the bet, "surrendering it," and keep the other half. This brings the house edge down to 2.63%.

American and European Roulette

The European and American game is pretty much the same besides the use of the French terms in Europe, and of course the American terms in the U.S. casinos.

However, there are two significant differences.

1. In addition to the 36 numbers on the roulette wheel, the American game has a 0 and 00; the European game has but one 0.

2. The European game offers en prison and partage, rules greatly beneficial to the player. En prison and partage is not offered in American casinos, with the exception of Atlantic City where surrender (partage) is used.

The end result, as we showed earlier, is that the casino edge in the European game is but 1.35% as opposed to American roulette where the player has to overcome a hefty 5.26% house edge (or 2.63% on even-money bets in Atlantic City).

THE WINNING STRATEGIES

First it must be stated clearly, that like most other casino games, the casino has the mathematical edge over the player. No betting strategy or playing system can overcome those odds unless the wheel is a biased one - which we'll cover.

That edge is 5.26% in American roulette, with the exception of even-money bets in Atlantic City where the edge is 2.63%, and 2.70% in European roulette, unless the even-money wagers are made, where the house edge drops to 1.35% on those bets..

Roulette Payoff Chart

Bets in Roulette

American Name	#	French Name	Payoff
Single Number	1	En Plein	35-1
Split Bet	2	A Cheval	17-1
Trio	3	Transversale	11-1
4-Number (Corner)	4	Carre	8-1
(Not Applicable)	4	Quatre Premiere	8-1
5-Number	5	(Not Applicable)	6-1
6-Number or Block	6	Sixaine	5-1
Columns Bet	12	Colonne	2-1
Dozens Bet	12	Dozaine	2-1
Red or Black	18	Rouge ou Noir	1-1
High or Low	18	Passe ou Manque	1-1
Odd or Even	18	Impair ou Pair	1-1

 # column is the amount of numbers covered by the bet.

Based on the above facts, one must develop a clear picture on how to approach a winning strategy.

First of all, it must be understood that in the long haul, thecasino's edge will grind out the player - but that doesn't mean the player can't show a profit in the short run. Fluctuations are normal to gambling, whatever the game, and with a little luck, a player can ride a hot streak into some healthy profits..

There are many betting systems that have been devised to overcome the casino's edge in roulette, but you must keep these in perspective, for they can no more alter or change the built-in house edge than one constantly calling a tree a river will change that tree to a river or calling blue red will change blue to red.

This is not to say that some of the betting strategies don't look good - some of them are brilliant in concept and *appear* fool-proof. As long as one realizes the risks involved and understands that no strategy can negate the built-in house edge, betting strategies can be a lot of fun.

Betting strategies can work - in the short run - and provide the player with a fun, working approach to winning, and really, that' s what the game is all about.

Let's look at one of the most famous systems first, The Martingale.

The Martingale

This dangerous system can dig you into a deep hole quick should you have a long string of losses - if not, like other systems, you'll be sitting pretty.

The system is easy. You attempt to win $1.00 on every sequence of the wheel, a sequence being defined as either one spin when you have won, or a number of spins, ending with a win.

Your first bet is $1.00. If the bet is won, you start again, betting $1.00. If you lose, the bet is doubled to $2.00. Should that bet be won, you have won $1.00 on the sequence, a $1.00 loss on the first spin a a $2.00 win on the second. If the second bet is lost, the next bet is again doubled, and is now $4.00. A winner here again brings a $1.00 profit, $1.00 + $2.00 in losers for $3.00 total, and a $4.00 winner. Still $1.00 over the top.

And so the system works. Every won bet is followed by a $1.00 wager, the beginning of a fresh cycle. Every lost bet is followed by a doubling of that bet. And here is the danger of the Martingale. As consecutive losses mount, so does the size of your bet, where the end result is only a $1.00 win!

This is what happens if you lose seven in a row.

Martingale Progression		
Loss	**Bet**	**Total Loss**
1st	$1.00	$1.00
2nd	$2.00	$3.00
3rd	$4.00	$7.00
4th	$8.00	$15.00
5th	$16.00	$31.00
6th	$32.00	$63.00
7th	$64.00	$127.00
8th	$128.00	-

Now suddenly, you're faced with a $128.00 bet with $127.00 worth of losses behind you. Now that's a lot of sweat and aggravation just to win $1.00 on the sequence. And we all know that seven losses in a row is not that strange of an occurrence.

What happens on the next spin? Surely you're due for a winner now after seven consecutive losses. If you're pregnant or expecting a raise or some such thing, you may be due.

In gambling, you're never due for anything. There are expectations based on the odds, but the fact that seven times the wheel spun black when you've been betting red, has no bearing on the eighth spin. The odds don't change - it's still an 18 out of 37 (European wheel) or 38 (American wheel) shot for your winning red on the next spin.

Remember, it's only a wheel. It has no memory, no brain. It doesn't know who you are, what you're betting, or that seven times in a row, black came up on it.

So back to the game. Heaven forbid that two more spins should go against you, for then you'll be faced with the following:

Martingale Progression Continued		
Loss	Initial Bet	Total Loss
8th	$128.00	$255.00
9th	$256.00	$511.00
10th	$512.00	-

Add up these numbers than get out the Pepto-Bismol. Think twice before using this classic system. Do you really want to risk a situation where you'll need to bet over $500 just to win $1.00?

The Grand Martingale

If you liked the above example, you'll love this system. The rallying point of the **Grand Martingale** is to attempt to win more than $1.00 on a losing progression by adding $1.00 to the bet after each loss. We'll spare ourselves the anguish of adding up these numbers, but you can see they'll add up even faster than the Martingale. Should things go badly, the bets get scary in a hurry.

The Pyramid System

This system is far more appealing to the player for its winning approach doesn't entail the kind of deep ditch digging that the Martingale and Grand Martingale do. In this system, also called the **D'Alembert**, we'll look at each bet it terms of $1.00 units.

The first bet will be $1.00. If we win, the sequence is ended, and we'll begin a new one. If the bet is lost, our next bet becomes $2.00. Each subsequent loss adds $1.00 to the bet, so that five consecutive losses would produce a $6.00 bet on the following play. (Compare this to the Martingale, where you'd be watching a $32.00 bet gracing the tables for your $1.00 win, and the first tinges of a headache beginning to pound your skull.)

This system is interesting for after every win, you'll decrease your bet by one unit! The end result is that every win (as opposed to every progression) produces a win of $1.00, or if you prefer to think in terms of units, every win produces a one unit gain.

Every won bet is $1.00 more than the previous lost bet.

Let's follow a progression to see how this works.

Pyramid Progression		
Bet	**Result**	**Total**
$1.00	Win	+$1.00
$1.00	Loss	$0.00
$2.00	Loss	-$2.00
$3.00	Win	+$1.00
$2.00	Win	+$3.00
$1.00	Loss	+$2.00
$2.00	Loss	+$0.00
$3.00	Loss	-$3.00
$4.00	Loss	-$7.00
$5.00	Loss	-$12.00
$6.00	Win	-$6.00
$5.00	Loss	-$11.00
$6.00	Win	-$5.00
$5.00	Win	$0.00
TOTAL - 14 Plays: 6 Wins, 8 Losses		

You can see the attractions of this system, for despite sustaining five straight losses and eight overall as against only six wins, the sequence where we left off showed the player dead even. A win on the next play would forge a profit of $4.00, with the next bet being $3.00, so the bettor's position looks pretty good overall.

This is all well and good on a short run look. However, in the long run, this system like all others trying to fight a game where the house has an edge, will ultimately lose. As the progression continues, there will be more losses than wins and the downward dips will be deeper and more frequent than wins.

As long as this is kept in mind, the immovable house edge, than one might play this system to great enjoyment, and in the short run, maybe some profit!

Biased Wheels

There is a way to beat the casino at roulette, but this involves finding an imbalanced wheel, presumably old and rickety, more likely in a smaller casino, or perhaps at a fair where the mechanics of the wheel are far from state of the art.

It is impossible to make a perfectly balanced wheel, one where each number has exactly the same chance of coming up as any other number. A slight imperfection in the material, normal wear and tear, a warp, a tiny tilt, an unlevel floor, a slightly larger or shorter slot - these possibilities or any of a number of others can cause an imbalance of a wheel and favor some numbers to be spun more than others.

Wheels are made with such tremendous precision nowadays that it is extremely unlikely to find a wheel with a bias significant enough to make this theory interesting.

However, you may find an older wheel in use, one that's been subjected to enough wear and tear of normal usage that a bias is created, or one with faulty mechanics, and until the casino has figured out that you've got something going on and shuts down the wheel, you can make a lot of money - with the odds.

First you must determine if the wheel is biased and how large the bias is. To do this requires a lot of work and patience, but if indeed you're hunch is right and the wheel is significantly biased, you will have made the effort worthwhile.

To properly track a wheel, you'll need a partner or an associate or two for every spin of the wheel will need to be recorded for at least 24 hours and ideally two or three times that much to get a fair sampling. A sampling taken for less than 24 hours will only show short run deviations (unless the wheel is incredibly biased) and will not be an accurate look at numbers which may be biased.

The expectation of any single number being spun is one in 37. For a bias to be effective and show profits, a single number's bias must not only be greater than the 1/37 expected result, but be sufficient enough to overcome the inherent casino's edge of 5.26% on an American wheel and 2.70% on a European one for single zero betting.

You may find one number or several that stand out on a wheel as being biased and base your winning strategy on those numbers (or number). The superior odds inherent in single zero roulette make those games much better to track for if a bias is found, the smaller house edge is easier to overcome and the profits will be greater.

PLAYING SLOTS TO WIN

INTRODUCTION

These ever-popular machines can be found around the world, buzzing, clanging and spitting out rewards to their faithful players. Millions are hooked on the game. Some play for the sheer pleasure, hoping to pass a little time and win a few coins, others play for that elusive thing, the big jackpot, which will set them on easy street.

Charles Fey is credited with being the originator of slot machines in their more or less current format. His original machines, called **Liberty Bells**, were introduced in the late 1800s and first began to appear in the bars and saloons around the San Francisco Bay. There were coin-operated machines before Fey which were based on games of chance such as dice and roulette, but Fey's Liberty Bell was the first to feature a three reel design with automatic payouts to the winners.

These early machines used three reels of ten symbols each, among which were the famous Liberty Bell figures, along with other symbols of the times such as horseshoes. If the 10 possibilities per reel are multiplied by three reels, 10 x 10 x 10, we come up with 1,000 different possible combinations on these early machines.

Fey set the machines to pay back 86% to the players. The other 14%, the profit, he split 50-50 with the bar and saloon owners. The machines really took off and spurred a host of competitors, most notably Herbert Stephen Mills and the Caille Brothers. Slots have come a long way since then and account for important parts of a casino's income.

Nowadays, the average slot machines accept 25¢ and $1.00 coins. However, some of the more plush casino offer their high rollers slot machines that take coins as large as $100 and even $500!

TYPES OF MACHINES

There are basically two types of slot machines. The first type, the **Straight Slots**, pays winning combinations according to the schedule listed on the machine itself. For example, one cherry may pay two coins for each one put in, two cherries may pay five coins and three cherries 10 coins.

The second type of machines are called **Progressive Slots**. These too have a standard set of payoffs listed on the machine itself, but in addition, and what sometimes makes for exciting play, is the big jackpot which progressively gets larger and larger as every coin is put in. The jackpot total is posted above the machine and can grow to enormous sums of money.

THE BASICS OF PLAY

Slots are easy to play. Machines generally take anywhere from 1 to 5 coins, and all one needs to do is insert the coins into the machine, pull the handle and see what Lady Luck brings.

There are many types of slot machine configurations but all work according to the same principles - put the money in the slots and pull the handle!

Often, the number of lines the machine will pay on depends on the amount of coins deposited. One coin only may pay the middle line, a second coin will pay the top line as well, a third coin - the bottom line, so now any of the three horizontals will pay should a paying combination be hit. A fourth coin may pay the diagonal, and a fifth, the other diagonal.

If the proper combination is hit, the machine should make a little noise for you as coins automatically pour into the well at the bottom. And should a really large payoff be hit, a jackpot, the machines will make a bunch of noise, a light may go off atop the machine and you just hang tight, for a casino employee should be there soon to give you the payoff.

More winning rows does not necessarily equate to better odds of winning. It just means more coins per play and therefore more possibilities of a payoff, for each coin gives you another bar or direction that will pay.

146

The odds are built into the machine and no amount of lines played will change them. The most important factor is how loose or tight the machines are set by the casino - that is what determines the odds facing a slots player.

Sample Slots Payoff (per coin)	
Winning Combination	**Payoff**
7-7-7	100 coins
Bar-Bar-Bar	50 coins
Bell-Bell-Bell	20 coins
Bell-Bell-Bar	18 coins
Bar-Bell-Bell	18 coins
Plum-Plum-Plum	20 coins
Plum-Plum-Bar	14 coins
Bar-Plum-Plum	14 coins
Orange-Orange-Orange	20 coins
Orange-Orange-Bar	10 coins
Bar-Orange-Orange	10 coins
Cherry-Cherry-Cherry	20 coins
Any-Cherry-Cherry	5 coins
Cherry-Cherry-Any	5 coins
Cherry-Any-Cherry	5 coins
Any-Any-Cherry	2 coins
Cherry-Any-Any	2 coins

SLOT PERCENTAGES

The percentage return of slot machines vary from casino to casino, and often within a casino as well. While the Nevada regulatory commission sets no minimum at all, the Atlantic City gaming commission requires a minimum return of 83% back to the players. Within these loose frameworks, a whole range of percentages may apply.

In general, a casino that relies on slots for a good portion of their income will offer players a higher return on their slots money, while those that have the slots as but an incidental income, will pay less on the average.

Some casinos advertise slots with returns as high as 97% to

the player, others, even as high as 99%! Obviously, the player stands a much better chance of winning at these places than others where a standard return of only 83% might be the norm. On machines in areas not covered by regulatory minimums, such as Nevada, players may not even get an 83% return.

SLOTS STRATEGY

The most important concept in slots is to locate the machines with the loosest setting, or with progressive machines, to play only the machines with the highest progressive setting.

The first thing to look for are casinos which really push their slot machine business and cater to the players, and also casinos which advertise a higher return. These are places that may offer slot players a better than average return.

In general, the poorer paying machines will be located in areas where the casino or proprietor hopes to grab a few of the bettor's coins as he passes through an area or waits on a line. Airport terminals, restaurant and show lines, bathrooms and the like tend to have smaller returns.

On the other hand, casinos that specialize in slots and look to attract serious players, will set up slots areas within a casino that will have better payoffs, or even, as you can find in Las Vegas, the whole casino will be slots only! These casinos view slots as an important income, and in order to keep regular slots customers, their players must hear those jackpot bells ringing - after all, winning is contagious!

Some machines are set to pay better than others, and these slots will be mixed in with poorer paying ones, so its always a good idea to look for the hot machine. Better yet, ask the change girls. They spend all day near the slots and know which machines tend to return the most money.

Basically, your best strategy is to examine the wide array of machines offered for play, and to find the best one suited to your personal style.

When you hit a good jackpot, make sure you set your stop-loss limit. This guarantees that you walk away a winner!

PLAYING VIDEO POKER TO WIN

INTRODUCTION

Video poker is fast becoming one of the most popular casino games. It's really a lot of fun, for decision-making and skill are involved and proper play can bring one profits. Even better, the game can be as leisurely or hurried as you want for there is no dealer to hurry you along. You choose your own pace - it's just you against the machine. May the best one win!

The whole setting is really simple. All one needs is some coins to play and an available video poker machine, and you're in business.

This section will show you the basic rules of play, the different games available, the payoffs at the various machines, and the best strategies to make you a winner.

Player Advantage in Video Poker!

There is another reason for video poker's increasing popularity and one players are slowly beginning to realize - you can actually have the edge over the casino playing video poker and like blackjack, have the expectation of winning money every time you play!

That's right, with proper strategy, you'll have the edge in video poker and if that isn't incentive to put a little study in the game and improve your odds, I'm not sure what is.

What we'll show you in this section is a simplified basic strategy that will improve your odds and get your game going in the right direction.

However, for those players serious about beating the house, you'll want to buy the advanced video poker strategy listed in the back. It takes you beyond the simplified basic strategy presented here and shows you the full Basic Strategy Charts, the advanced strategies, which machines to play for best results and overall, how to be a winner and play video poker for a profit.

THE TYPES OF MACHINES

Video poker offers the player a variety of machines from which to choose. The two basic types of video poker machines are the **Flat-Top** (or **Straight**) machines and the **Progressives**. The Flat-Tops offer set payoffs on all the hands won, with the payoffs proportionately larger for greater amounts of coins played. Thus, a winning payoff on two coins played will be exactly double that for the same winning hand with one coin played.

The one exception is for the royal flush, where a winning payoff will give the player a 4,000 coin return when five coins are played, as opposed to only 200, 400, 600 and 800 coins on a one, two, three and four coin play respectively. All other payoffs are in proportion.

Winning payoffs are posted on the machine, so you can see right off what you're up against.

The Progressive machines differ from the Straight or Flat Tops in that when a royal flush is hit with five coins played, the payoff is not a set amount but is based on a progressive total. This jackpot constantly increases until the royal is hit, when it will start again at a set amount, such as $1,000 on a 25¢ machine.

The Progressives can be exciting for jackpots go higher and higher, and now and again, a quarter machine will soar well into the $2,000+ range or even higher. However, like the Straight machines, the full five coins must be played to reap the full reward when the royal flush is hit.

There are different varieties of the video poker machines within the above classifications. A player may find Jacks or Better, 10s or Better, Deuces Wild and Joker Wild, and these can be played as Straights or Progressives, depending upon what casino players find themselves in and what machines are offered.

HOW TO PLAY

Video poker is basically played as draw poker. The machine uses a 52 card deck which is played fresh after each hand. While you won't receive the same card within a play, for the machine will deal cards from the 52 card computer pack, the memory ends there as the deck is "reshuffled" after each deal.

To start, you need to insert anywhere from one to five coins into the machine. The choice is yours - play one or play five at your discretion. We will recommend that serious players insert the full five coins to get the best odds, but we'll go into that later.

If five coins are inserted, the machine will automatically deal a hand to you. However, if less than the maximum amount is inserted, you'll need to press the button marked **DRAW/DEAL** to receive your cards.

Five cards will show on the screen. These are your cards. You may keep one, some, all or none of the cards. It's your decision. To keep a card, press the button marked "**HOLD**" underneath the corresponding card you wish to keep. There will be five hold buttons, one for each card, and for each card you want to keep, you must press the hold button.

"HELD" will appear on the screen underneath each card or cards so chosen. The other cards, the ones you wish to discard, will not be kept by the machine.

What happens if you press the wrong hold button by accident or change your mind? No problem. Press the corresponding button again. If the card indicated "HELD," it will no longer do so and will not be kept by the mcahine. If you again change your mind, press the button one more time, and the "HELD" sign will come on the screen indicating that the card will be kept.

Until you press the draw button, it is not too late to change your strategy decision.

You may keep all five original cards by pushing the hold button under each card. You may also discard all five original cards if so desired by *not* pressing any of the hold buttons.

You now press the DRAW/DEAL button to receive new cards. The "HELD" cards will remain and those cards not chosen to be held will be replaced with new ones. This set of cards is the final hand.

If your hand is a winner, the machine will flash "**WINNER**" at the bottom of the screen. Winning hands are automatically paid according to the payoffs shown on the machine.

Winning Video Poker Hands

Jacks or Better - Two cards of equal value are called a pair. Jacks or better refers to a pair of Jacks, Queens, Kings or Aces.

Two Pair - Two sets of paired cards, such as 3-3 and 10-10.

Three of a Kind - Three cards of equal value, such as 9-9-9.

Straight - Five cards in numerical sequence, such as 3-4-5-6-7 or 10-J-Q-K-A. The ace can be counted as the highest card or the lowest card in a straight, however, it may not be in the middle of a five card run, such as Q-K-A-2-3, which is not a straight.

Flush - Any five cards of the same suit, such as five hearts.

Full House - Three of a kind and a pair, such as 2-2-2-J-J.

Four of a Kind - Four cards of equal value, such as K-K-K-K.

Straight Flush - A straight all in the same suit, such as 7-8-9-10-J, all in spades.

Royal Flush - 10-J-Q-K-A, all in the same suit.

Five of a Kind - Five cards of equal value, a hand that is only possible in wild card versions of video poker. For example, if deuces are wild, the hand 2-2-7-7-7 would be five sevens.

Credit

There is a useful feature offered on many video poker machines that allows you to play on winnings using a credit function built-in to the machines.

Let's say for example, that you've just hit a win for 20 coins. Two things will happen. On the machine, you'll see "Credit - 20" appear. To continue playing without cashing out and reinserting coins, you can now press another button that will have lit up and be indicated by the label, **Maximum Bet**, **Bet 5** or some similar name. This allows you to play five of your 20 credits toward a new hand which will appear on the screen along with the information that your credit now stands at 15.

The second thing that will happen after your 20 coin win is that a button called the **Cashout** or **Payout** button will light up. If pressed, the machine will give immediate payment of the winnings registered in the credit area.

The Cashout button can be used after any hand is completed to cash out wins that have accumulated, or if you want to continue playing on credit, keep pressing the Maximum Bet button to get a new hand dealt.

The hands in the chart below are listed in ascending order, from weakest to strongest, as they are in the payoff charts in this section, with the exception of the Five of a Kind hand, which is usually stronger than a Royal Flush composed of wild cards but weaker than the Royal made naturally - without wild cards.

JACKS OR BETTER: 9-6 MACHINES

These machines are known as **9-6 machines**, because of the 9 and 6 coin payouts when the Full House and Flush are hit. Note that a pair of 10s will not pay anything back, nor will any lower pair. A hand of jacks or better is needed for a payout.

Payoffs on Jacks or Better · 9-6 Machine					
Coins Played	1	2	3	4	5
Jacks or Better	1	2	3	4	5
Two Pair	2	4	6	8	10
Three of a Kind	3	6	9	12	15
Straight	4	8	12	16	20
Flush	6	12	18	24	30
Full House	9	18	27	36	45
Four of a Kind	25	50	75	100	125
Straight Flush	50	100	150	200	250
Royal Flush	250	500	750	1000	4000

Progressive Payout

Besides the straight machines discussed above, there are Progressive machines, as in slots.

All payoffs, like the straight machines are fixed except in the case of a Royal Flush, where this grandaddy pays the accumulated total posted above the machine on the electronic board. This total slowly, but constantly rises, and on a quarter machine in Las Vegas can rise into the thousands of dollars.

The following chart shows typical payoffs for video poker on a Jacks or Better Progressive machine. This machine is known as an **8-5 machine**, so named for the payoffs given on the full house and flush respectively.

Payoffs on Jacks or Better · 8-5 Progressives					
Coins Played	1	2	3	4	5
Jacks or Better	1	2	3	4	5
Two Pair	2	4	6	8	10
Three of a Kind	3	6	9	12	15
Straight	4	8	12	16	20
Flush	5	10	15	20	25
Full House	8	16	24	32	40
Four of a Kind	25	50	75	100	125
Straight Flush	50	100	150	200	250
Royal Flush	250	500	750	1000	*

*When five coins are played and the royal flush is hit, the bettor receives the full amount accumulated for the Progressive jackpot. Note that all five coins must be played to win the jackpot.

10S OR BETTER VIDEO POKER

The 10s or Better machine is only found infrequently. The following is the payout on the non-progressive machines. Note that Royal Flushes pay 800-1 only if five coins have been played.

Payoffs on 10s or Better					
Coins Played	1	2	3	4	5
10s or Better	1	2	3	4	5
Two Pair	2	4	6	8	10
Three of a Kind	3	6	9	12	15
Straight	4	8	12	16	20
Flush	5	10	15	20	25
Full House	6	12	18	24	30
Four of a Kind	25	50	75	100	125
Straight Flush	50	100	150	200	250
Royal Flush	250	500	750	1000	4000

WILD CARD VIDEO POKER

Two variations of video poker that have caught on and gained in popularity are the **Deuces Wild** and **Jokers Wild** machines. Wild cards can be given any value or suit and the machine will interpret wild cards in the most advantageous way for the player.

For example, the hand 2 2 5 6 8 in Deuces Wild would be a straight, for one 2 can be used as a 7 and the other as either a 9 or 4. The deuces could also be used as eights to give three of a kind, but since the straight is more valuable to the player the machine will see it as a straight.

Wild card machines have different payoff schedules than the Jacks or Better machines, and these machines will start giving credit only on a three of a kind hand or better.

DEUCES WILD VIDEO POKER

Deuces Wild is played the same way as the Jacks or Better and uses the same standard 52 card deck, but in this version there is one important difference - the four deuces (2s) are wild, and can be used as any card in the deck, even to make a five of a kind.

The video poker machine will recognize the best hand possible using the deuces and will automatically give credit for the maximum hand value that can be made.

Deuces Wild Video Poker Payout					
Coins Played	1	2	3	4	5
Three of a Kind	1	2	3	4	5
Straight	2	4	6	8	10
Flush	2	4	6	8	10
Full House	3	6	9	12	15
Four of a Kind	5	10	15	20	25
Straight Flush	9	18	27	36	45
Five of a Kind	15	30	45	60	75
Royal Flush (deuces)	25	50	75	100	125
Four Deuces	200	400	600	800	1000
Royal Flush (Natural)	250	500	750	1000	4000

Note that the Royal Flush as a natural hand (without the deuces) will be paid off at 800-1 only if five coins are played.

JOKER WILD VIDEO POKER

There are two version of the Joker Wild game: **Ace-King** and **Two Pairs**. In the Ace-King version, a minimum hand of a pair of kings must be made for a payoff. In Two Pairs, two pair is the minimum hand needed for a payoff.

Both versions of Joker Wild are played with a 53 card deck, the regular 52 card deck plus the wild card, the **joker**, which can be assigned any value. Keep in mind that the Royal Flush will only be paid off with the maximum return if five coins are played.

Joker Wild Video Poker Payout · Ace-King					
Coins Played	1	2	3	4	5
Ace or Kings	1	2	3	4	5
Two Pair	1	2	3	4	5
Three of a Kind	2	4	6	8	10
Straight	3	6	9	12	15
Flush	5	10	15	20	25
Full House	7	14	21	28	35
Four of a Kind	20	40	60	80	100
Straight Flush	50	100	150	200	250
Royal Flush (Joker)	100	200	300	400	500
Five of a Kind	200	400	600	800	1000
Royal Flush (natural)	250	500	750	1000	4000

Note the same payout whether one gets a pair of Aces or Kings, or Two Pair.

Some machines pay off only 15 for 1 on the four of a kind instead of 20 for 1 as shown above. Give these machines a miss.

Note that five coins must be played, and should always be played, to receive the maximum payout for the Royal Flush. For example, the Royal Flush will pay out 4,000 coins or $1,000, for a quarter machine when five coins are played, while four coins would yield only 1/4 as much - $250.

Getting a Straight Flush with five coins will pay 250 coins or $62.50 and a Full House will pay 45 coins or $11.25 for that same quarter machine.

Joker Wild Video Poker Payout · Two Pair					
Coins Played	**1**	**2**	**3**	**4**	**5**
Two Pair	1	2	3	4	5
Three of a Kind	2	4	6	8	10
Straight	5	10	15	20	25
Flush	7	14	21	28	35
Full House	8	16	24	32	40
Four of a Kind	20	40	60	80	100
Straight Flush	50	100	150	200	250
Royal Flush (Joker)	50	100	150	200	250
Five of a Kind	100	200	300	400	500
Royal Flush (natural)	250	500	750	1000	4000

WINNING STRATEGY

The big payoff on video poker machines is for the royal flush. It doesn't matter what variation is played - Jacks or Better, 10s or Better, Deuces Wild or Joker Wild - a whopping 4,000 coins are paid for this big daddy when five coins are played. And on progressive machines, if a full five coins are played, the total could be a great deal higher, making the game even more interesting for the player trying to land himself or herself a jackpot to remember.

Of course, the royal doesn't come often. With correct strategy, you'll hit one every 30,000+ hands on the average. This doesn't mean, however, that you won't hit one in your very first hour of play!

But meanwhile, you'll be collecting other winners such as straights, full houses and the like, and with proper play, all in all, you can beat the video poker machines. To win, you must play the correct strategies. Like regular poker, there are skillful ways to play your hand.

However, unlike regular poker, you're not playing against other players, but against a machine, and the strategies must be adjusted accordingly. Strategies that make sense in the Friday night game may not be the proper ones at a video poker machine.

Always Play Five Coins

To achieve the absolute best odds at the video poker machine, five coins must be played. At first glance, this suggestion probably strikes you as being strange. Why not one coin or two? After all, the payoffs on all hands at the video poker machine are proportionately the same whether one, two, three, four or five coins are played.

However, there's one glaring exception - the royal flush. And though this hand doesn't come often, it does come and much more so than in a regular poker game for we're playing an entirely different strategy in video poker. We're concentrating on the big score, the royal flush, as opposed to a regular poker game, where you primary goal is simply to win the hand, even if a pair of sevens do the trick. And in video poker, a pair of sevens is worth nothing - the machine gives no payoff for it.

We're playing the odds at the machines, and you'll find yourself throwing away hands that you would never do in a regular poker game. But like we mentioned above, video poker is not a regular poker game.

Look back at the payoff chart for Jacks or Better. Notice what happens on the royal flush payoffs. Interesting, yes? One coin played returns 200 coins, two coins yields 400, three coins 600 and four coins brings home 800 bad boys. Well, the progression for the fifth coin should be 1,000 if you're following along with the addition. But it's not.

The full payoff on a royal flush with five coins played is 4,000 coins! Now that's a nice payoff and that's also the reason we're going to be playing five coins. The royal is not as remote as it seems. You may never see one in a regular poker game, but at the video poker machines, following the strategies we suggest, you have a good chance to stare one in the face as the ringing bells mesmerize your gambling psyche.

You'll see similar jumps for the Royal Flush payoffs on all the video poker machines.

Therefore, to collect the full payoff on a royal flush, proper play dictates that you always play the full five coins for each game. For if you do hit the royal flush, there's a big, big difference between 1,000 coins returned and 4,000 returned.

Of course, players who want to play less seriously can play any amount of coins from 1 to 5 and still enjoy the game.

Find Machines With the Best Payoffs

The payoff schedules we've listed in this section are not the only ones you'll find for the games we've discussed. There are machines with less generous payouts as well. When possible, always choose machines with better payouts. For example, when there is a lot of casino competition, such as Las Vegas, a little window shopping will definitely be to your advantage.

Winning Strategy for Jacks or Better

Following are some basic strategy principles for the jacks or better machines:

1. Whenever you hold four cards to a royal flush, discard the fifth card, even if that card gives you a flush or pair.

2. Keep a jacks or better pair and any higher hand such as a three of a kind or straight over three to the royal. Play the three to a royal over any lesser hand such as a low pair or four flush.

3. With two cards to a royal, keep four straights, four flushes, and high pairs or better instead. Otherwise, go for the royal.

4. Never break up a straight or flush, unless a one card draw gives you a chance for the royal.

5. Keep jacks or better over a four straight or four flush. Also, keep low pairs over the four straight, but discard those pairs in favor of the four flush.

6. Never break up a full house or four of a kind. Also, don't break up two pair and three of a kind hands. The *rags*, worthless cards for the hand, should be dropped on the draw.

7. The jacks or better pair is always kept, except when you have four cards to the royal, or four to the straight flush.

8. Low pairs are broken up in favor of a four flush (but not a four straight) or when dealt three or four to a royal flush. Otherwise, keep the low pair and draw three fresh cards.

9. When dealt five odd cards, save in order, four flushes, four straights, three to a straight flush, two cards to the royal, two cards jack or higher, one card jack or higher. Discard the odd cards, the rags in these hands.

10. Lacking any of the above, with no card jack or higher, discard all the cards and draw five fresh ones.

Simplified Basics Strategy Chart

The following chart sums up the simplified basic strategy for Jacks or Better. The hands are listed in order of strength from most powerful first, the Royal Flush, to the least powerful last, the garbage hands. Keep the hands listed higher in preference to hands listed lower. For example, you'll keep a High Pair over a three to a royal, but throw it away in favor of a four to the royal.

Jacks or Better - Simplified Basic Strategy Chart		
Hand to Be Held	**Cards Held**	**Cards Drawn**
Royal Flush	5	0
Straight Flush	5	0
Four of a Kind	5	0
Full House	5	0
Four to a Royal	4	1
Flush	5	0
Three of a Kind	3	2
Straight	5	0
Four to a Straight Flush	4	1
Two Pair	4	1
High Pair	2	3
Three to a Royal	3	2
Four to a Flush	4	1
Low Pair	2	3
Four to a Straight	4	1
Three to a Straight Flush	3	2
Two to a Royal	2	3
Two High Cards	2	3
One High Card	1	4
Garbage Hand - Draw Five	0	5

Winning Strategy for 10s or Better

10s or Better is played similarly to Jacks or Better, except that you should keep a pair of 10s instead of discarding them for they yield a payoff.

Otherwise, follow the strategy as outlined above in Jacks or Better Winning Strategy.

Winning Strategy for Deuces Wild

Deuces are extremely valuable cards so when you get them, make sure you never discard them by accident. You'll notice that there is no payoff for hands less than three of a kind, so our strategy must be adjusted accordingly.

The key in Deuces Wild as in the non-wild versions is to go for the big payouts - the royal flush. Therefore, when you have three cards toward a royal flush discard the other two and go for it. Of course, the same holds true when you have four to the royal. Thus, if you have two deuces and a 10 or higher, along with two sub-10 cards of no value, go for the royal.

Similarly, if you have two deuces and three cards below the 10 in value, dump the crap and hang onto the deuces, unless two of the cards are paired in which case you have four of a kind, or the two cards retained give you four cards toward a straight flush.

If you hold one or two deuces with nothing else that's interesting, dump the junk and hang onto the deuces. If you're hand is really poor, and you're dealt five unrelated cards, get rid of them all and go for five fresh ones.

Three card flushes or straights are worthless in this game as are single unmatched high cards so don't be holding onto hands of this nature. You'll also get rid of two pair hands - for they don't pay. Hang onto one of the pairs, and go for three new cards.

If one of the pairs is teamed with a wild deuce, keep the three of a kind. However, if the deuce forms a high pair, it does no good at all and as suggested above, keep the deuce and draw four new cards.

Keep a pair at the outset, unless you've got a three card straight flush or royal flush going, in which case you'll dump the pair and go for the gold.

You'll find that many of the hands you'll be dealt will contain nothing worth saving and you'll be drawing for five fresh cards. Three card straights and flushes fit in this category along with some of the others we've mentioned. In any case, don't be afraid to discard your original five cards if they hold nothing of value.

It will take a little while getting used to wild card video poker after playing the non-wild versions, but once you get accustomed you should have a lot of fun at these machines.

Making Money at Video Poker

Video poker is certainly a fun game, for it is a game of skill, and as we stated in the beginning, with proper play you can have the edge over the casino. Like blackjack, you need to study the correct strategies carefully to come out a winner, but a little preparation can payoff in winnings.

For those players serious about moving forward in the game, the professional video poker strategy advertised in the back is highly recommended. It is the strategy used by professional players who earn their living at the video poker machines. You'll learn the important differences in strategy between the 8-5 Progressive and 9-6 Jacks or Better machines plus receive *complete* strategy charts for these games, the wild card games, and others.

Meanwhile, use your skill to good advantage, and see if you can't beat the house and be a winner!

MONEY MANAGEMENT

Winning at gambling requires not only the playing of the correct strategies but also the intelligent use of one's monetary resources. Preparation is key.

To emerge a winner from the streaky swings of fortune inherent in gambling takes a certain degree of emotional control, for the temptation to ride a winning streak too hard in the hopes of a big killing or to bet wildly during a losing streak, trying for a quick comeback, can spell doom.

Big winning sessions can dissipate into small wins or even disastrous losses while moderately bad losing sessions can turn into a nightmare.

Money management is the most important factor in the winning formula, so don't gloss over this section. Without these skills, you cannot win at gambling, even though the odds may favor you. So give this a good read, and take our advice seriously.

If you do, you'll find yourself on the money end of the table, as a winner, and that's what our goal in gambling is all about!

Money management skills can be divided into the following three categories:

- **Emotional Control**
- **Bankrolling** (Total bankroll, table bankroll).
- **When to Quit** (Maximize gains, minimize losses).

Before we look at these skills more closely, there is one extremely important point that must be thoroughly understood.

Never gamble with money you cannot afford to lose either financially or emotionally.

Betting with money you cannot afford to lose adversely affects decision making. Rather than playing your best game, your strategy gets restricted to the confines of your monetary or emotional situation, rather than your intelligence and skill.

Betting with "scared money" is a guaranteed way to ensure yourself a losing career as a gambler.

EMOTIONAL CONTROL

It is important to recognize that behind every bet you make is your money and your emotions, and that the ups and downs of your moods and feelings affect the quality of your play.

Sometimes you won't feel 100%, perhaps a day where your confidence or alertness is low. Whenever you feel emotionally unprepared to risk money, again, you should refrain from playing. And if, for whatever reason, the game becomes a cause of anxiety and ceases to be a form of entertainment, than it is time to take a breather.

You won't play as well because your mind will be preoccupied by the possibility of losing and perhaps more importantly, you will receive no emotional satisfaction from the game.

Play again later on, when you're more alert and confident, and you will have the necessary ingredients of a winner - emotional control. Remember, the casinos aren't going anywhere. There's lots of time to get your bets down.

For gambling to be a pleasurable and successful experience, you must *feel* like gambling *and* must be able to afford possible losses, emotionally as well as financially.

BANKROLLING

To be a successful player, your bankroll must be large enough to withstand the normal ups and downs that are the very nature of gambling. Under-capitalization and overbetting leaves a player vulnerable in two ways.

First, a normal downward trend can wipe out a limited money supply. Second, and more important, a player feeling pressured by limited capital will play less intelligently than smart play dictates. And that is where you start giving the odds back to the casino and playing like a loser.

The key to winning is to play for the win and that means smart money management - using your head. If the amount staked on a bet is over your level, you're playing in the wrong game. Play only at levels of betting you're comfortable with.

Minimizing Losses

Here are three simple guidelines that, if followed, will save you a lot of money.

1. Limit your table losses.

Do not dig in for more money, and you can never be a big loser. As they say, the first loss is the cheapest. Take a break, try again later. You never want go get into a position where losing so much in one session totally demoralizes you.

2. Never increase your bets beyond your bankroll range.

In other words, always bet within your means.

3. Never increase your bet size to catch up and break even.

Raising your bets will not change the odds of the game, nor will it change your luck. What it will do is make your chances of taking a terrible beating frighteningly high. As we discussed earlier earlier, do not get into a position where losing so much in one session destroys any reasonable chance of coming out even. You can't win all the time. Rest awhile; you'll get 'em later.

WHEN TO QUIT - MAXIMIZING GAINS

What often separates the winners from the losers is - the winners, when winning, leave the table a winner, and when losing, restrict their losses to affordable amounts. Smart gamblers never allow themselves to get destroyed at the table.

As a player, you have one big advantage that, if used properly, will insure you success as a gambler - You can quit playing whenever you want to. To come out ahead, you must minimize your losses when you lose and maximize your gains when you win. This way, winning sessions will eclipse losing sessions and overall, you'll come out a winner!

Let's move on now to the games themselves!

THE GRI MASTER KENO STRATEGY
David Cowles Professional Winning Strategy

Finally! David Cowles, the *world's foremost expert on keno*, and the publisher of the *Keno Newsletter*, has released his **powerhouse strategy** on winning money at keno **exclusively** to Cardoza Publishing. This strategy is now available for the **first time** and is only available through us!!!

TIRED OF LOSING? LEARN HOW TO WIN! - Learn how to bet the tickets that provide the **highest payoffs** and push the percentages in your favor, how to increase winning tickets **tenfold** using way, combination and king tickets, how to set goals and plot a winning course, how to parlay small bankrolls into large fortunes by **playing smart** instead of betting haphazardly, and how to stretch your bankroll so you have **more winners** and chances for **big jackpots**!

WIN MORE PLAYING KENO! - Cowles reveals, for the first time, the magic *wager-to-win ratio* - a quick way to determine if a keno ticket is playable; also how to find the most **profitable** tickets, the *real scoop* on how to **pick winning numbers**, tips from the pros on **winning** keno tournaments and contest prizes.

THE SECRET TO THE MOST PROFITABLE BETS - Many keno tickets are blatant ripoffs. Learn to avoid the sucker bets and how to **slash the casino edge** to the bone. You can't change the odds, but you can get the best deals once you learn the *secrets* revealed here.

FREE ROOM, FOOD & DRINKS? - You bet! They're yours for the taking. You just have to know *who, how* and *when* to ask - and then *how much*.

DOUBLE BONUS! - With your order, **absolutely free**, receive two insider bonus essays: *12 Winning Tips From the Pros* - the 12 master jewels that can increase winnings drastically; and *The 10 "Don'ts" of Keno*, mistakes made by both novice and experienced players. You'll never make these mistakes again. Be a winner!

To order, send $50 by check or money order to Cardoza Publishing

168

GRI'S PROFESSIONAL VIDEO POKER STRATEGY
Win Money at Video Poker! With the Odds!

At last, for the first time, and for serious players only, the GRI Professional Video Poker strategy is released so you too can play to win! You read it right - this strategy gives you the mathematical advantage over the casino and what's more, it's easy to learn!

PROFESSIONAL STRATEGY SHOWS YOU HOW TO WIN WITH THE ODDS - This powerhouse strategy, played for big profits by an exclusive circle of professionals, people who make their living at the machines, is now made available to you! You too can win - with the odds - and this winning strategy shows you how!

HOW TO PLAY FOR A PROFIT - You'll learn the key factors to play on a pro level: which machines will turn you a profit, break-even and win rates, hands per hour and average win per hour charts, time value, team play and more! You'll also learn big play strategy, alternate jackpot play, high and low jackpot play and key strategies to follow.

WINNING STRATEGIES FOR ALL MACHINES - This comprehensive, advanced pro package not only shows you how to win money at the 8-5 progressives, but also, the winning strategies for 10s or better, deuces wild, joker's wild, flat-top, progressive and special options features.

BE A WINNER IN JUST ONE DAY - In just one day, after learning our strategy, you will have the skills to consistently win money at video poker - with the odds. The strategies are easy to use under practical casino conditions.

FREE BONUS - PROFESSIONAL PROFIT EXPECTANCY FORMULA ($15 VALUE) - For serious players, we're including this free bonus essay which explains the professional profit expectancy principles of video poker and how to relate them to real dollars and cents in your game.

To order send just $50 by check or money order to:
Cardoza Publishing, P.O. Box 1500, Cooper Station, New York, NY 10276

PLATINUM "PLUS" LOTTERY/LOTTO™

Prof. Jones' Pro Level Computer Strategy - **For Serious Players** (IBM and Mac)

NEW REVISION! - The **king** of Lottery/Lotto software has gotten even better! New revision includes Power Ball, Summation Analysis/Charts, Last Number Recall, Wheel Optimizer. Use this super-powerful and versatile system to play and beat 3 and 4 number lottery; five ball, six ball, power ball or bonus ball lottos. Unique user-friendly "click and pick" creates scientific wheels quick and easy - let the program do the work! Only lotto program featuring **Artificial Intelligence!!!** The Platinum Plus includes all the goodies of the Mini-Platinum Plus **and more**, and is for players **going for the max**!!!

SUPER STRATEGY - This **super strategy** features **over 20** of the Dimitrov Systems, the Hard Positional Analysis, all the Cluster, Bell, % of Occurrence, % of Frequency, Past Winning Numbers, Two Digit Numbers and lots more!

MORE FEATURES! - This **awesome** strategy features an **expanded** cluster analysis, skip/hit chart, **hot number** & regression analysis/testing, *unlimited* wheeling systems! **Very powerful**, excellent **top-of-the-line** strategy! Includes hardbound manual, 90 day after-purchase support & replacement warranty with optional 1 year extension, and is backed by more than **ten years of customer satisfaction**!

HOT NUMBER ANALYSIS:
Using the skip hit chart, numbers are based on their overdue status.

SKIP HIT CHART
A true "TIME ORIENTED" sequence to allow you to actually see when each ball was picked.

EXPANDED CLUSTER ANALYSIS
The Cluster Analysis looks at first and second clusters, 3 through 20 picks.

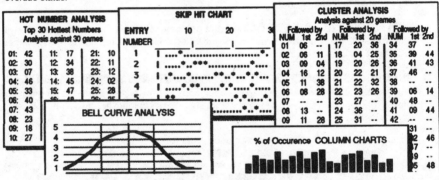

To order, send $149.95 by check or money order to:
Cardoza Publishing, P.O. Box 1500, Cooper Station, New York, NY 10276

170

174

Look for some great upcoming games - *Avery Cardoza's Slots* (with 100 slot machines), *Avery Cardoza's Blackjack*, and *Avery Cardoza's Poker*. We'll be bringing you great entertainment!

Check out our web site at:
www.CardozaEnt.com

Important!
Send in Your Registration Card Now!